Timeless Teaching Tips

by Joyce Herzog

joyceherzog.com
1-800-745-8212

© 1999, 2002
by Joyce M. Herzog

All rights reserved.

No part of this work may be reproduced
or used in any form by any means –
graphic, electronic, or mechanical including
photocopying, recording,
taping or information storage and retrieval systems
without written permission from the publisher.

ISBN 1-887225-20-X

joyceherzog.com
1-800-745-8212

Printed in the United States of America

Timeless Teaching Tips
Table of Contents

INTRODUCTION

PRINCIPLES OF LEARNING

Learning is Basic	1
Teaching	5
Think Like a Teacher	5
Steps of Good Teaching	9
Find a Bridge	19
Is it Knowledge or a Skill?	23
Learning	27
Learning Enhancers	27
Children Have Needs	34
Differences in Children	40
Labels Limit	43
Increasing Creativity	48
Learning Within the Family	51
Goals and Goal Setting	51
Do: Involve: Explain	56
Principles of Changing Behavior	59
What about Commitment, Respect and Obedience?	67
Grandma Scares Me, Too	73

Table of Contents, Continued

IT'S BEEN SAID

Introduction	79
Education	81
America as A Nation	82
Science	92
Worldview	94
God and The Bible	95
Important Quotes of Famous People	97

PRACTICAL HELPS

Limited Resources	103
A Dozen Teaching Tips	111
Teaching with Homeschool Notebook Journals	120
Thoughts on Reading	124
Teaching Reading Comprehension	130
Adult Reading Difficulties	135
Building Spelling Success	138
Math Helps	141
About Rewards	148
Including Young Children in the Homeschool	151

HOMESCHOOLING ISSUES

Happy Helpful Hints	161
Get a Jump Start!	167
MultiLevel Can be Fun and Easy!	170

Table of Contents, Continued

GEMS
Children	179
Learning Differences	193
Teaching	197
Parents	210
Training Character	213
Christian Training	215
School	221

SPIRITUAL CONSIDERATIONS
How do I Bring My Children Up in the "Fear and Admonition of the Lord?"	225
Soaking in the Scriptures	227
Understanding the Bible – The Big Picture	230

Obeying Your Parents According to the 90's Generation

Children, obey your parents,
    if they promise great treats and rewards.

Children, obey your parents,
    but roll your eyes and make a face
    so they know you don't like it.

Children, obey your parents,
    but first tell them all the reasons
    you think it is unreasonable to do so.

Children, obey your parents,
    if and only when you really feel like it.

Children, obey your parents,
    but do so grudgingly, haltingly, and as slowly as possible.

Children, obey your parents,
    but only after you tell them all the things you had planned to
    do just as soon as you got around to it that must definitely be
    done before you could be available to do what they want.

Children, obey your parents,
    as soon as you have finished contemplating the existence of
    trees, work, man, life, the stars and all other questions
    in your mind.

Children, obey your parents,
    but only when they tell you to do something
    you already wanted to do.

Children, obey your parents,
    but do a horrible job of it
    so they'll never ask you to do it again.

Children, obey your parents,
> *after* you have told them how unreasonable they are to expect you to do so.

Children, obey your parents,
> *if* it is convenient and happens to be something you wanted to do already.

Children, obey your parents,
> *but* put it off till later.

Obeying Your Parents According to Definition

Obedience is pleasant, quick cooperation. If it is not pleasant **or** not quick **or** not cooperation, it is a form of rebellion, however subtle. Subtle rebellion is just as deadly as out and out disobedience.

Obeying Your Parents According to the Bible

Children, obey your parents in all things: for this is well pleasing unto the Lord.

— Colossians 3:20

Conclusion:

Children, obey your parents!

Principles of Learning

Learning is Basic

Learning is basic. It is natural. Learning begins in the womb and continues until it is no longer rewarding. The job of a teacher is to create an environment in which learning continues to be rewarded and rewarding. **Good teaching is providing opportunities and an environment in which learning can occur.** Good teaching is a delight both to the student and the teacher. Bad teaching is equally frustrating for both.

God made us to learn. Very few 20-year-old adults are still lying in a cradle wearing diapers and drinking from a bottle.

> **God made us to learn.**

They have learned other options. The ones who are still at that stage have, for the most part, been brain-injured in some horrendous accident. God made us to learn - not even just ready to learn. We are learning even before birth, and unless we deliberately choose not to, we continue learning throughout our lives. God created us to learn. That's the good news. Our children are learning every day, whether or not we are deliberately teaching them. That can be scary! What we, as

⇨ Timeless Teaching Tips

teachers, want to do is direct their learning in ways that will be beneficial.

Did you ever think about what you are teaching when you aren't even thinking about it? If, when you see a worm, you say yuck and grimace, what are you teaching about worms, the Creator God, and small, harmless creatures? If, when you hear thunder, hear a severe windstorm, or see a tornado, you respond with tension and fear, what are you teaching about nature, storms, and God's protection? If you frequently ask a 2-year-old, "Do you like it?" what are you teaching him? If you tell him frequently, "You don't like eggs," what are you planting in his mind? Little children are mimics. They are watching you and learning from you when you least expect it. Lead them carefully and prayerfully.

Teaching is a decision-making process. What shall I teach Johnny today? What materials should I use? How should I present the materials? What should I do if he resists? What will I have in the background if he doesn't understand? How will I evaluate whether he has learned? How often should I review? How can I help him see the relevance of this concept to his everyday life? How will he practice the skill? How will he apply the principles learned? How much can I expect to cover in one session? How often should I introduce a new concept? Where will I find the materials I need? Is there a field trip we can take to reinforce this concept? Oh, and he is just one of my seven children... What about Mary? Danny? Susy? Steven? Betsy? And the baby! It's too much unless you organize and simplify!

Principles of Learning

Good child rearing requires distancing ourselves from our own needs. As long as our primary focus is on our own desires, we will have little time left over to observe or meet the needs of our children. On the other hand, if all our focus is on pleasing our children, our own needs will be neglected leading to lack of health and energy to meet any needs. As usual, balance is the key. Another key is in carefully recognizing the difference between wants and needs.

The atmosphere in the learning environment is far more important than your chosen curriculum, though the two are often intertwined. Children can not learn in an atmosphere of fear, anxiety, tension, confusion,

> **Optimum learning depends on the atmosphere.**

great physical discomfort, or even anticipation. They must feel accepted, valued, and capable for optimum learning to occur. It is important to encourage each child to try - and to accept mistakes as a part of life. Each mistake shows you something that doesn't work. That is valuable learning. Allow your child to explore. Does he have any time to explore? Does he have the skills to explore? Are interesting materials available to explore? Can he have your attention occasionally to help him profit from his explorations?

Good learning environments provide opportunity for questioning and assists in locating answers. It presents information in ways that are interesting and invite exploration. It fosters an atmosphere where new ideas are allowed and all are willing to learn from the others. Yet, for things to still run smoothly, there needs to be a clear authority who safeguards

⇨ Timeless Teaching Tips

against danger, time constraints, and other restrictions and emergencies.

Children learn. It is the responsibility of the teacher to enhance the opportunities for learning and direct the maturation of thinking and reasoning skills.

Principles of Learning

Teaching

Think Like a Teacher

A friend once asked me if I could teach her how to think like a teacher. I had never thought about it. It took some thought, but here are some of the things I have learned that make a difference.

It is essential that you speak to the children like they are a person, not just like a child. It is a matter of tone, body language, and

Children are people.

choice of words. They must know that you recognize them as persons separate from yourself - persons with opinions, skills and preferences. They need to know who is the ultimate boss (you!), but there are many times when it is appropriate to ask their opinions and preferences.

Whenever it is possible to do so, offer a choice. In this way the child will learn to make decisions, have an

Offer a choice

opportunity to express his desires, and be led to cooperate. When there is no choice, make that clear in a non-threatening way. Here are some possible scenarios:

➡ Timeless Teaching Tips

• We're getting dressed. Would you like to wear the blue outfit or the red?

• It's time for breakfast. Would you like toast or cereal?

Don't ever offer (with your words or tone) a choice if there is none. "Would you like to go to bed now?" is only appropriate if they are allowed to say, "No!" "Get dressed now, okay?" means they have a choice. "Do you want to pick up now?" may get the answer of, "No!" "Why don't you come over here and sit down?" may get the appropriate answer, "I don't want to."

Take them one step further.

When your children were infants, it was natural to start where they were and stretch them one step further. You did not say, "He is two days old, he should be looking left and right and kicking his hands and feet." You did (though probably subconsciously) start taking them one step at a time toward developing listening skills, attention span, muscle tone, visual skills and so on. Continue throughout life. Determine the area where you want to see progress, and the present level of ability. Set goals that are well within reach and reward amply for reaching for them or meeting them. If you are looking for help in identifying the next step in various areas, look at the author's books *Luke's School List* (kindergarten through eighth grade academics) and *Luke's Life List* (list of skills based on Luke 2:52 including early childhood, wisdom, stature, favor with God, favor with man, and adult life skills).

Principles of Learning

Don't take the easy way out. It is natural to want to take the easy option, but both in parenting and in educating, it is often essential to do what is tough, but beneficial.

Don't take the easy way out.

Give your children time to struggle without help or condemnation. Speak clearly and say what you mean. Make sure that you are clearly understood. Make it easy to succeed. Reward the truth. If you give an order, see that it is carried out. Don't demand where options are acceptable. When there is disobedience, respond immediately. Don't look the other way unless you want them to learn to ignore you next time.

Encourage mature language.

Encourage them to use mature and precise verbal language. Ask them to describe details they can see. Later ask them to describe details they can't see at the moment. You will need to begin this by asking appropriate questions. If they answer with one word, restate their answer in a sentence. Encourage recalling and retelling stories and events. Assist with getting things in sequence, stating information in complete sentences, transitioning smoothly from one idea to the next and using descriptive and interesting words. When checking for comprehension, ask open-ended questions like "Why?" and "How?" Ask them to define words. Encourage the verbalization of thinking and the development of steps and plans.

⇨ Timeless Teaching Tips

Listen to your child.

When a child asks a question, determine what he knows already. It is easiest to just begin talking, but more efficient to listen for a few moments to discover what information (or misinformation) he brings to the topic. Then, take him a step or two further. It is often best to answer a question with a question, "What do you think?" "How could you figure that out?" etc. Wait at least three seconds after asking a question before going on with an explanation. Children need time to formulate their answer - and they may take longer than we.

Have fun!

Thinking like a teacher really comes down to knowing where you want to go and choosing which way to get there, who to take on the journey, and how long to allow. You can do it! Have fun!

Principles of Learning

Steps of Good Teaching

All good teaching should include some basic steps:
- **Introduction**
- **Model**
- **Instruction for Practice**
- **Guided Practice**
- **Independent Practice**
- **Application or Project**
- **Report: Written or Oral**
- **Review**
- **Evaluation**

⇨ **Timeless Teaching Tips**

Introduction

1 The introduction is a way to whet the appetite to learn more about a topic. Presenting the "big picture" is usually a part of the introduction. The introduction should provoke interest, arouse the curiosity, raise questions, and leave questions unanswered. The introduction should present a purpose for learning which appeals to the felt needs of the learner. Most children learn better if they sense the meaning of the information. Many need to see the whole to have a place to "hook" the pieces. Children need to own the problem before they are interested in the solution.

> **Start with the Big Picture**

During an initial talk with the children, have everyone share what they already know about the topic. This can be done before or after a very basic introduction such as reading aloud a picture book. Make a list of what they know and what questions they still have. Use that information to help guide your teaching plan and your plan for evaluation (making up a test).

Principles of Learning

There are many ways to introduce a new topic. Reading aloud a picture book is my favorite. It is a fun way to give the big picture. Picture books are colorful, pleasant and often give some new information while they review what is already known about

Ways to Introduce a New topic

the topic. They help the older learners see things in perspective and probably contain enough content for the younger learners. Sometimes a map, diagram or a chart is a great way to begin. A discussion of important terms may open a new topic. Ask thought-provoking questions to spark interest. Old textbooks, encyclopedias or magazine articles may be just the springboard you need. A trip to a play, a museum, or a historical place related to the topic is fine. Children love board games, and there is probably one on the market for almost any topic you choose. Look at some objects or replicas related to the topic.

Model

2 The second step of good teaching is to model the type of behavior you expect the children to perform. Hopefully, this is a natural part of your relationship already. You may want to demonstrate possibilities or show what someone else has made, done, or written about the topic. If the subject is math, work some problems and discuss the steps. Show something someone has made related to the topic. Take the children to a museum or class performance that demonstrates the type of behavior you hope to see them develop. Show a finished project. This will spark ideas. Some will want to mimic what they have seen; others will want to do something along the same line, but with

⇨ Timeless Teaching Tips

their uniqueness. Others may react by moving in an entirely new direction. All of these responses are normal and good. If you expect the child to write a report or do a science project and he has never before seen one, you have put him at a gross disadvantage.

Guided Practice

3 This is the step which is most often compromised and at times even skipped altogether. It is not wise to merely move from demonstration to assignment. Work with the student until he is comfortable and at least

> **Guide his practice until he is working successfully and independently.**

somewhat sure of himself, gradually turning over the control. First, teach. Then repeat, leaving out some essential parts. Next, question to see if the child has the steps or facts necessary to work independently. Then have the child direct as you carry out the necessary steps. Finally, when he seems to be confident, send the student to work independently.

In arithmetic, have the student state the formula. Let him dictate the steps while you do the work. Allow the student to work through the steps under your watchful eye. Gently redirect as he makes errors. Remember, the first time you do anything, you need a little extra help and harsh criticism is not helpful. Whenever possible, find a formula, state it simply, and repeat it frequently. If the child is doing math problems, check each answer for accuracy until the student gets three in a row right, then have him immediately do a few independently. The next

Principles of Learning

day he may need more guided practice before he is able to work independently again. Some children will need this approach of review followed by a bit of independence for several days in a row.

In the content areas such as history, science, and so on, gather materials at a variety of levels - above and below each student's level as well as right at his level. Use picture books, games, biographies, coloring books, well-written novels, encyclopedia articles and non-fiction books at all levels. Have each student do some general reading (easy-for-him reading level). Use picture books to intrigue, interest, and see the main points. Read some aloud, leave others for the children to read to each other or independently. Ask questions related to what they've read to help them see there's more to it. Before asking them to do research, have them define the object for their research. Have them state the topic they will research and list questions they will seek to answer.

Independent Practice:

4

On my own at last.

Finally the student is competent to try to work all by himself. In arithmetic, the student now works problems without assistance or encouragement. In history, science, and so on, the students are ready to learn on their own. They may read, fill out workbook pages, create projects, or do research. As they read and research, encourage them to take notes on 3x5" cards

⇨ Timeless Teaching Tips

and record the source of the information. They could file the note cards by topic in a file box. This is excellent preparation for independent research in high school. Provide opportunity for them to interview persons who know about or work in the field of topic. This could be done as a group interview, with each ready with a question or two. Tape record the session to review later.

Throughout the study, encourage your learners to share frequently what they're learning. Help them identify what is important and needs to be remembered and what they need to research further. Assist students as needed, but encourage increasing independence.

Application or Project

5

> **Let me show you what I know.**

It is not enough to merely know the information. There needs to be opportunity to share what is known with an audience. Frequently the class or family is the only audience you need. Homeschoolers may like to have a weekly time when Dad gets involved and talks with each child about what he is learning. This not only builds family, it also gives the student an opportunity to become teacher. The best way to learn is to teach because it forces clarity. The need for an audience can also be beneficial for public relations. Classes sharing within a school build bridges of learning and understanding. Most

Principles of Learning

homeschooling families have neighbors, relatives, or friends who do not understand or encourage homeschooling. Once a month, or at the end of an exceptionally good unit, plan for a special night and invite a class or family and friends. Serve a meal or snack related to the topic. Show photos of trips and projects which have been organized and labeled. Perform a play, skit, or reading. Allow each person to "show and tell" something they made or learned. Take photos, too, of the event itself. Afterwards, have the children make a scrapbook or collage as a remembrance.

In arithmetic the real application of a skill is to use it in story problems. If the student cannot use the skill in story problems, he has probably memorized a series of steps with little or no understanding. Math is useful only when it relates to life. After "school" is over, there will be no more math tests, but there will be innumerable times in life where the adult needs to know how to apply math to real life. As in any other topic, it is important to work together at first. The amount of time this requires decreases with the learners ability to handle things independently.

Teach your learners to verbalize their thinking as they work through a story problem. Show ways to draw a picture of the concept. Substitute little numbers which clarify the problem. Do this until the student is comfortable working on his own. This will differ with the age and maturity of the learner and from subject to subject and day to day. Do not assume if he can work independently today, that he will remember perfectly tomorrow. He may need several days of success before he is ready to work without any assistance.

➡ Timeless Teaching Tips

Finally your student must be encouraged, or even forced, to work through problems on his own without help. The final step is for the student to write story problems of his own. He may need some help setting up the problem at first, but eventually he will likely find this to be the most fun!

In history, science, and so on, the student should **make** something to show that he has learned. Some suggestions are for him to make a model, diorama (shoebox scene), puppet show, miniature or working model. The subject may lend itself well to a diagram, a three-dimensional map, a graph or a chart. Artistic children may want to create a poster or collage, a cartoon or a book. A radio or t.v. ad, a play a poem, or a song may be enjoyable for some. Most children would find it fun to play a (board) game or take a field trip related to the subject. It is important that the child get immersed and involved in the topic.

Report: Oral or Written

6 The report is the finale. It should always be included, but in a variety of ways. It may be as simple as explaining and demonstrating the project or papers he has completed.

> **There are many ways to report.**

At other times, it may be to give a two to twenty minute speech, write a story, one or several paragraphs or a three-page report. Older students should learn to develop a twenty-page report complete with illustrations, bibliography and footnotes. Some students will be able to write or perform a skit or play. Some may choose to read or recite something they have written or someone else has produced. Children of any age

Principles of Learning

can make or write a book. This can be done at many levels - from dictating a word or sentence per page and then illustration it to writing illustrating and binding a full-length book. A wonderful culmination is to teach another child or adult. Don't neglect those opportunities when they come.

Review

7

Review can be fun.

If the material is to be learned for life, almost constant review is essential. Variety is the key to review. If the only method used is oral recitation, boredom soon sets in and hinders learning. Some of the review can be incorporated into or an extension of the project stage. The child could make a game or write a play that reviews the important concepts. He might tape record questions and answers and then listen to the tape several times. One student might write a test for another. Flash cards, with the answer written on the back, might be made for almost any subject. These could then be incorporated into a boardgame, with two correct answers required to earn a turn. Many children love to use highlighters and can be taught to look for the key ides and phrases. Posters and collages can show a conglomerate of ideas about a topic. Outlining is a helpful skill as well. The important thing is that key concepts be culled out and recited in various ways. Some children need more review than others. Adjust this phase accordingly.

 **Timeless Teaching Tips**

Evaluate

8

See what I've learned.

Evaluation can be informal or formal. It can be related to the project or report, or it can be a separate test administered in a formal setting. It is important, too, to know what you are evaluating. If you are grading for history, do not take off for sentence structure. On the other hand, you may read a paper or test in history and give a history grade and a language grade or give both a math grade and a handwriting grade for a page of completed problems. A grade can be based on percentage of information assimilated, quality of ideas expressed, amount of effort expended, application made, or a combination. Ideally what is being graded should be communicated at the outset, not after the grade is determined. Whether or not you issue a formal grade, one of the best teaching techniques is feedback. The student needs frequent assurance that he is making progress and meeting goals. Charts are good to see a visual representation of progress.

My husband often says that he was graded, not on what he knew, but on how fast he assimilated it. Often students' grades are based on how fast they can communicate what they know. They may also reflect the manner in which the text was given. Some auditory and verbal students are actually downgraded because they must give answers in a written form. More rarely students may be able to do better writing than speaking. When a grade is a necessity, make sure that it is an accurate reflection of what the student has actually learned.

Principles of Learning

Find a Bridge

Most children know "everything there is to know" about something they are interested in. That may cause you to say, "If you really wanted to, you could learn ____." And you are right. There is an important key principle there: We all learn more easily when we are interested in the topic at hand.

Most children have a special delight in some topic. It may be dinosaurs, baseball, trains, or motorcycles. It may be sports, automobiles, costumes, bridges, or Legos™. Or music, or horses or kittens. You are probably already naming the thing your child is particularly interested in. You're thinking, "Sure, if we could talk about ____ all day long, my child would be perfectly happy. But we can't."

Maybe you can. Let's take a lesson from the Master Teacher: Jesus. When he was talking to farmers, he talked about seeds and soil and seasons... things farmers were familiar with. When he was talking to fishermen, he talked about nets and fishing, and boats. But he

Learn from Jesus.

19

⇨ Timeless Teaching Tips

didn't teach them more about the things they knew. He only used that as a jumping off point. He started from what they were interested in and found ways to relate that to what He wanted to present: the Kingdom of God. We can do the same thing. Think of what your child is interested in. Find ways to jump from that to what you want him to know. Here are some samples to get you going.

Say your child is interested in motorcycles and you want him to learn to multiply. How many wheels does one motorcycle have? How many wheels on four motorcycles? Or ten? The two-times table are easy picturing motorcycles. Let's add a side car to each motorcycle and picture the three times tables. Six couples (each on their own motorcycle) are buying new tires (or handle grips). How many will they need? What about two couples, or eight couples. Now you are doing the fours (two couples are four people) and you are seeing that the fours are double the twos. How can we do the fives? Well, if five motorcycle clubs have a party and each one orders three pizzas, how many pizzas will the restaurant need to cook? If each pizza feeds (2, 4, or 6) people, how many people can each club feed? How many people can eat altogether in the five clubs? You can go on from there.

If your child loves sports, music or dress and you want to teach him history, follow the development of his love through the ages. Read biographies of people involved in the topic he has interested in. Let him try to duplicate the game, music or costume of the period you are studying. If your child loves trains and you want him to study history, look at the history of transportation - the development of trains and the prior developments that led to the invention of the steam engine. That

Principles of Learning

just may lead to a discussion of science and how steam and scientists have affected history.

If he loves automobiles and you want him to study science, look at the principles of science that were involved

Relate learning to your child's delights.

in the development of the automobile. Look at simple tools like a wheel, lever and screw and see how they were put to use in the design and manufacture of cars. Steam cars and tractors were followed by the gasoline engine. Battery operated cars have been tried. What is to be the fuel of the future? Now you're studying history, science, and inventions... and because you've related it to your child, he's loving it! Read and write about it and you've covered the language arts as well.

If he wants to be a doctor and you want him to study language, have him read a biography of

Keep a journal.

Ben Carson. Remind him that someone had to know and remember what Ben Carson was like as a child to write a biography of him. Encourage him to keep a journal now so that someone in the future can write a biography of his life and include accurate facts and feelings. Voila! Painless practice with writing.

Find biographies related to the subject he loves and you've easily integrated reading and history. Have him write a letter to a person, living or dead, who was involved with the subject and you've covered language. Or have him write a diary as if he were there. Or a description or instruction on how to make or use or where to buy the thing he is fascinated with. Math may be

➪ Timeless Teaching Tips

measuring or figuring out how long ago things happened or keeping track of baseball averages. Use your imagination. Find a bridge between what you want him to learn and where he is. You'll both find learning more interesting... while your child makes more progress than ever!

Principles of Learning

Is it Knowledge or a Skill?

There is an error afoot which can only be corrected by coming to some understanding of a very important but subtle difference - the difference between skill and knowledge. A skill must be developed gradually, but knowledge can be acquired instantly.

Knowledge in a Moment - Skill in a Lifetime

A skill involves learning to do something, learning to apply a principle or committing large number of facts to memory. Cooking is a skill. Knowing the difference between slicing and chopping or between baking and frying is knowledge. Playing the piano is a skill but learning which is the treble clef and which is the bass clef is accumulating knowledge. Both are important, but they must be approached differently. z

Approach each Differently

If you want to learn to play the piano, you can't do it all in a day. It will take years of practice. Proficiency will take many years of practicing for an hour or more every day. If you want

⇨ Timeless Teaching Tips

to know which key signature has only one flat, you need only ask.

> **Skill - bits of information, chunks of practice**
> **Knowledge - chunks of information, bits of practice**

To teach a skill, give a small amount of information and allow a big time for practice. Teach great chunks of related knowledge in a short amount of time. To do that, it is important that you determine whether you are teaching a skill or knowledge.

Some skills we want to develop are learning to read, learning any new language (spoken or written), learning to use a new or unfamiliar tool such as an electric saw or a microscope, learning to outline, and memorizing anything: facts, definitions, Scriptures. Other skills are learning to sew, draw, gain physical skill and strength, and developing all artistic talents: music, drama, dance or visual arts. These take small practice sessions accumulated over a long period of time.

Acquiring knowledge includes such things as studying history; finding out the three branches of government, learning the parts of a flower, or learning about sound, oceans, or music theory. You can know the states and their capitals, the parts of the body, the way the body systems work. It may take time to memorize many facts, but you can become acquainted with them in a matter of minutes.

Principles of Learning

> **Acquire Knowledge within Context**

Acquiring knowledge is best and most easily done when information is presented within a fun or familiar context, such as a story or an activity. Acquiring knowledge fits well into the unit study or real book approach to learning. Knowing is finding out about, becoming acquainted with, meeting. Accumulating knowledge may take time if there are many small isolated facts to memorize, such as the addition facts or the state capitals. That becomes a skill itself and relies heavily on the skill of memorization. We, unfortunately, assume children can memorize automatically and rarely take the time to teach or develop that skill.

The key to memorization is frequent regular doses of repetition with variety. To aid your child in acquiring knowledge, teach him to memorize.

Here are some hints:

• Group related pieces of information.

• Repeat frequently in two ways:
<u>hearing or seeing</u> exactly the same thing daily or even several times a day
<u>stating the idea</u> in different words or showing it in a different context

• Tape record the full information (question and answer, statement and source, all parts of a play, problem with solution, etc.) and listen to it frequently while you are busy doing

25

⇨ Timeless Teaching Tips

something else and when you are giving it your full attention. You can even use this as you drop off to sleep.

• Tape record (the question without the answer, prompt without your part, source without statement, etc.). Play it and try to fill in the missing part.

• Use rhythm or rhyme, catchy phrases or intriguing pictures.

• Repeat the information during rhythmic body movements like doing jumping jacks or marching.

• Make up an acronym using the information to be memorized. An acronym uses the first letter of each part of the information to spell a word or easily remembered sequence.

• Use associations (sounds like..., looks like..., etc.)

Memorization and other skill development fits well into daily doses of a half hour or less. Meeting new ideas is more appropriate for a unit study approach inundating the child(ren) with related information in an active context.

Before you decide how to teach a given subject or fact, determine whether it is a skill or knowledge. Then go about it in the most appropriate way. Happy learning!

Principles of Learning

Learning

Learning Enhancers

Let's look at some ways to enhance learning.

Both movement and rhythm are natural ways to improve learning for most children. For some they are almost essential. I

> **Let me move and sing.**

discovered in the fourth grade that if I paced back and forth while reading out loud, I memorized faster and retained it longer. Many children profit from bouncing on a mini tramp as they recite math facts or spell words. If you can put the facts needed to learn into a rhyme or song, they will be infinitely easier to assimilate. Some children are particularly adept at this and can be encouraged to make up rhymes and songs which all may then learn. There are also many learning songs on the market.

> **Make it colorful.**

Color can be used in a variety of ways that benefit learning. Writing each fact in a different color ink, or on a different color paper can make it easier for some children to learn. Others

⇨ Timeless Teaching Tips

learn better if they can choose their favorite color for a fact which is difficult for them. Illustrating the concept through drawing, doodling, graphing, and so on is beneficial for many learners.

Organization of thought is an excellent learning aid. Ideas can be arranged chronologically, in either ascending or descending order of importance, or in alphabetical or numerical order. Making an acrostic sometimes helps, like **A R**at **i**n **T**he **H**ouse **M**ay **E**at **T**he **I**ce **C**ream helps children learn to spell *arithmetic* and an acronym like **HOMES** is can help you remember the Great Lakes: **H**uron, **O**ntario, **M**ichigan, **E**rie, and **S**uperior. Encourage the children to find these little "handles" themselves. It greatly improves their attention to details. Associations can help too, though they are actually a hindrance for some who can remember the association, but not what it was associated with!

> Teach me to organize.

Body position and **physical comfort** also affects learning. It is hard to study and learn when you are cold or wearing a scratchy sweater. Some children are more affected by this than others, but I remember as a child being absolutely unable to think when a tag on a dress or blouse was itchy. I have seen boys who think better with their legs above their heads, and girls who prefer lying on the floor. There are times, of course, for

> Consider my comfort.

Principles of Learning

decorum, but other times when those preferences can be considered.

Keeping fingers busy helps some children's minds to think more freely. Some children have great difficulty focusing attention on the subject at hand.

> Some need busy fingers.

They may concentrate on everything at once, or on nothing at all. Often keeping their hands or mouths busy with some mindless activity increases their ability to take in information, especially when listening is necessary. Chewing gum or sucking on candy may actually help them concentrate. Other mindless activities, such as manipulating and twisting something, stacking blocks, drawing or coloring may free the mind to listen.

Some people, like myself, actually improve learning by talking. My brain processes things I have not even thought of dealing with. I love to listen to the words that come out of my mouth and am

> I talk to learn what I think.

sometimes amazed at the clarity of thought and intensity of the ideas they reveal. Preplanned speaking is important for many. When we are forced to verbalize ideas, we have to figure out what we think, organize and prioritize the details, and find a way to present them in a way that the listener will stay interested long enough to hear the conclusion. That really requires much mental assessment and contemplation and increases the likelihood that we will remember the information. This can be especially helpful when it is one who learns by

⇨ Timeless Teaching Tips

talking can be paired with one who needs auditory presentation or a great deal of repetition.

Being questioned often encourages and even forces clarity of thought beyond the ordinary. Most of us don't think until we are questioned about *what* we think.

> **Ask me what I think.**

> **Start with overview.**

It is a good idea to start by giving a quick overview. Do not make the mistake of giving the whole lesson twice and calling the first presentation an overview. The overview should hit only the very most important highlights and provide a place to hook the coming details.

If the topic is historical, showing where it fits on a timeline is also helpful, but give some hooks to the timeline as well. This can be done through color coding (green for Old Testament Times, red for New Testament, brown for middle ages, etc.) through specific hooks (like Creation, Abraham, David, Jesus, Vikings, Pilgrims, Patriots, Pioneers and Me), or through colors or symbols (different ones for scientists, artists, historians, financiers, politicians, etc).

Principles of Learning

> **I don't understand those words.**

It is essential to make sure that the important vocabulary words are fully understood before going deeply into any subject. It is true that some vocabulary can only be understood within the context of the subject, but there are other vocabulary words that must be understood before getting very far into the subject.

> **All things in order.**

Adopt some sort of orderly system for presentation. This can be chronological, from cause to effect, from simple to complex, from the inside out, from mundane to the heartfelt. You've got the idea. The more organized the presentation, the better the retention.

Anther aid for retention is the old familiar KISS (Keep it So Simple!). Three points is ideal. Four points around a central highlight (five in all) is excellent. Examples are important, but be careful that they are truly related to the topic. It is easy for the examples to become the focus and the point is forgotten.

> **Keep it so simple.**

⇨ Timeless Teaching Tips

Children - and many older learners as well - learn best by doing. Hearing the information is the least effective, seeing it better;

> **Let me do it, please.**

physical involvement the best. Doing something with the information can be as simple as drawing a picture, map or chart, or as complex as putting on a full play about the topic. In between are such activities as making a model, outlining, creating a poem or story, impromptu acting out of the action, and making and labeling a diagram.

Hearing information is greatly enhanced if it is presented in such as way as to be visualized. This will require skill on both the part of the teacher and the student. The

> **If I see and hear and do, I learn.**

teacher must use word pictures: detailed description, rich metaphor (implied comparison like "an ocean of tulips") and simile (stated comparison using like or as, for instance, "as green as grass" and "like a red red rose"). The student must be given opportunity to develop skill wholesome visualizing. This is done normally as you read aloud. At first the young child has many pictures and is constantly looking at them as you read. As his interests mature, there are fewer and fewer pictures and they are shown less and less frequently. This both allows and forces the student to "see" the story in his own mind. Movies and videos tend to lessen or destroy this skill. When a video of a book or story is seen **before** the story is heard or read, usually

Principles of Learning

only the scenes of the movie are visualized. This actually limits creativity and thinking.

It is essential to relate new concepts to some thing the child already knows or understands. It is hard to remember isolated bits of information because there is no way to categorize them. "Hooking" the new to the old is a great way to enhance understanding and memory. Tell the child what it is like.

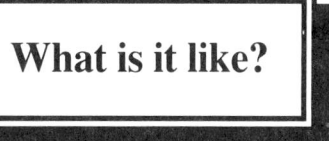

These memory and understanding enhancers are invaluable in increasing the learning for most of us. When they are left out, much of our learning becomes temporary - learning for the test without absorbing the concepts for life. Such learning has little use in real life.

 **Timeless Teaching Tips**

Children Have Needs

Considering the built in needs of children is important. It frees us to work in mutually beneficial ways. It also keeps them happier, and anyone who works with children knows that happy children learn better and make more progress than pressured ones (not to mention being more pleasant to have around!). Let's look at some key needs of most children.

> **Children need to move.**

Children have a need to move. We need to build action into the way they can respond to what we ask them to do. Instead of always using paper and pencil, let them manipulate magnetic letters. Instead of saying yes or no, have them clap or jump. Or allow a wiggly active moment in between two quiet studious times. For example, if the situation demands that the student listen, think and give an oral response (like mental math, spelling words, or reciting facts), have her first stand quietly to listen and respond. Then, if the answer is correct on the first try, allow a physical response. Have her do a jumping jack, touch her toes, or run around the

Principles of Learning

table. If the answer is correct on the second try, allow a slightly less physical response. She may bend from the waist, clap her hands, or kick one foot. The next week let her sit on the floor to listen and jump to her feet for a correct response. Plan for variety! Keep things moving!

Children have a need to receive attention from the adults in their lives. In many homes children are clamoring in

> **Children need attention.**

inappropriate ways for attention. They whine and wiggle and hit and cry. They get on our nerves and **then** we give them attention! Unfortunately by then it is negative attention and everyone is upset and unhappy. Children really need attention. It is our job to give them positive attention **before** they demand attention in negative ways. Spend a few minutes after breakfast in controlled planned activity - whether your child is six months old or six years old. By then they'll probably be only too happy to play quietly on their own. Make sure they have appropriate playthings. That does not necessarily mean the newest most colorful and noisiest toy on the market. It may be the measuring spoons and cups and a box of dried coffee grounds or colored cornmeal or crayons, markers, paper and scissors.

Children need lots of opportunities to "do it all by themselves." Whenever possible, rather than doing things for them,

> **Children need to do it.**

let them do it even if it takes longer and the results are not as neat. If you always do it, when will they hone their own skills?

⇨ Timeless Teaching Tips

Sometimes they learn valuable lessons by trying the impossible. Sometimes they succeed in **doing** the impossible! On the other hand, they will never even do the possible if they are not allowed to try. They must learn that it is okay to try and fail. It is okay to try and succeed. It is not okay to never try. Give them the time and space they need to grow.

> **Children love variety and repetition.**

While most children thrive on variety, they also love frequent repetition of their **favorite activities**. Plan for both. With young children have a four-week rotation of some favorite but messy activities, like painting, clay, cooking, and projects. Each week (perhaps only one day in the week) allow the activity of the week. Use it as a reward if you like, but don't let too many weeks go by without it. Have some activities that you do every day, like reciting a scripture at breakfast, singing a song at lunch and sharing something you learned at supper. Each day try to have one activity that you haven't done for several days, like jumping on the trampoline, doing aerobics, or working on a project.

> **Children forget.**

Children forget. Even though you thought the child totally understood and saw that he could apply a concept one day, he may not even recall that you talked about it the next. Start with a quick review of the process and be delighted and surprised if he remembers **anything!** Build up from simple to complex each day especially in math and spelling

Principles of Learning

to give success and increase confidence. Plan to spend a week to a month reviewing at the beginning of the school year if you have taken a break of a month or more. Also plan for shorter times of review after other breaks - for instance, after a weekend, a holiday, or an illness.

> **Children don't need frustration.**

Many children have a low tolerance for frustration. They do **not** learn from frustration. Limit the time of struggle and gradually build up their tolerance for struggling with a difficult task.

For example:
- If math is a struggle, have him do five math problems. If they're all correct that's it for the day. If not, work the next two with the child and then have him do one alone. The next day do five more of the same kind and try it again.

- Sandwich difficult struggles between two lighter, less demanding activities. If the child struggles to write, do a reading, drawing or listening activity first and then limit the writing to ten or fifteen minutes. Give the child a choice of writing materials. Follow the writing by a short break and then working on a project.

- Set a timer for ten minutes. If he works hard for that ten minutes, give him a five-minute break before another ten-minute work period. If he doesn't, set the timer for another ten minute work period. After two such failures, switch to a different learning activity, but do not allow a "break."

▶ **Timeless Teaching Tips**

• Each day dictate ten words, allow a wiggle break and then dictate two sentences. Small doses repeated regularly lead to steady progress.

> **Children need success.**

Children need success. If they don't find success doing what you ask of them, they will succeed at being the troublemaker, the clown, or the pest. You control what a child is asked to do each day. Don't let the demands of any specific curriculum dictate to you. If a child is constantly unsuccessful, you need to take charge. Break the task down into smaller steps that he can conquer - or back off and give him time to mature. Children who find success in small ways every day will have amazing ability to tackle enormous challenges.

Children need the same break we would give to a stranger. If a friend who is visiting spills a drink, we smile, shrug it off and wipe it up. If our child does the

> **Children need a break.**

same thing, do we react the same way? Actually it might be better to have your child wipe up his own spill, but without recrimination.

Principles of Learning

Not all days go well. If the day has been absolutely the pits, take a mental break and find a way to redeem the day.

> **Redeem the day.**

Drop the unsuccessful plans and blow bubbles in the back yard, pop popcorn and watch a video, pack up a lunch and picnic at a park, or just hug and tickle and giggle for a few minutes. Don't let a day end in despair - for you or the children. Remember, they are not just your charges - the kids you have to raise: They are your brothers and sisters in Christ! Remember the built-in needs of your children and enjoy this opportunity to experience and to express God's love and forgiveness!

⇨ **Timeless Teaching Tips**

Differences in Children

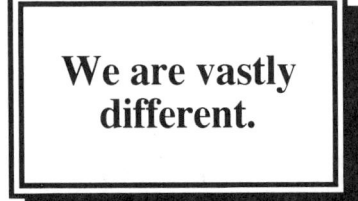

We are vastly different.

Many families have two or more children with vastly different learning patterns. Perhaps the younger child learns everything quickly and easily. You tell him once and he's got it. He's good at everything he does, and he does everything. The older child struggles to learn. He has to have everything presented ten times in 20 ways before he even begins to grasp it. Even then what he grasps today he often forgets by tomorrow. This older child may watch his brother soar through the very lessons that bring him to his knees. He may begin to withdraw and resist learning. To compound the matter the younger boy may have no patience with his older brother, and they may seem to have nothing at all in common.

Is it possible to work with all in the family in ways that will draw them together?

Principles of Learning

All children were created by the same loving God. He didn't make a mistake on one of them. He has a purpose for each one. We have to

God made us all.

remember that ourselves and remind our children of that in many ways as well. Pray for God's guidance.

Ideas that work.

Here are some other things that might help:

• 1. Find things the struggling learner is good at and give him all the praise he can handle.

• 2. Let him learn something from a friend or relative that is unknown by the more gifted sibling. Then let the struggling learner teach that topic to the faster learner.

• 3. Read aloud some biographies and study the characters of people who have struggled against difficult odds to carry God's call on their lives.

• 4. Make sure you genuinely praise each child in private and in front of the other. Do not choose favorites. Remember Joseph and his brothers!

• 5. Teach the siblings to help each other and cheer the other's progress. Show them this by your example, by being proud of each and giving them opportunity to shine.

⇨ Timeless Teaching Tips

• 6. Realize that children need to be taught character, attitudes, and values far more than they need lessons in academics.

• 7. Enjoy each of your children for what they are and what they become. Let them know often what you appreciate about them. An accepting atmosphere makes it easy for them to see and copy accepting attitudes!

• 8. Study God's perspective of character, talents, and stewardship. For a start, note how Jesus treated people with problems. Then look at the very different personalities that were needed to do very different jobs in the Bible and more recent history. Moses the plodder verses Joshua the conqueror, and quietly persistent Albert Schweitzer versus dynamic Martin Luther. It is our differences that make us interesting and helpful to each other. Begin to celebrate our uniqueness!

Principles of Learning

Labels Limit

All kinds of labels can limit our children's ideas about who they are and what they can become. If "he's the scientist," then she doesn't believe in her ability in science. Actually she may have more ability - or just the right combination of ability and determination - to become a scientist. She may never explore enough to discover that! One mother I talked to said when she was recently thinking of taking art lessons, she called her sister to ask permission! Her sister was "the artist" in their family and she felt guilty even thinking of dabbling in the forbidden area! Scenarios like that could fill this book!

I had to think long and hard about an alternative way to describe children, introduce them, and even speak to them about their talents and abilities, likes and dislikes, and weaknesses and strengths. I finally came up with some good ideas about what to do. The biggest problem then becomes how to change. We are deeply entrenched in the old methods. Let's look at a different approach and give some thought to making a change.

➡ Timeless Teaching Tips

Avoid labels.

When you describe a child, whether you are talking to them or about them, avoid labeling. Both good and bad labels can be destructive. Often they cast children into a mold which may become uncomfortable as the child matures. We must learn to communicate and describe without labeling. To learn how to do this, we are going to have to think about transitive and intransitive verbs. Transitive verbs are verbs of action: likes, makes, does, jumps, runs, goes. Intransitive verbs are verbs of being: is, was, were, and so forth.

Intransitive verbs (verbs of being) are the troublemakers here. When used to describe a person, they refer to the very being -- the very essence -- of the child. Use them to describe innate, unchangeable qualities that cannot be disputed. Do not use them to describe likes and dislikes, temporary strengths or weaknesses, or even tendencies. It is okay to say, "Johnny is the third-born child." No one can argue with that and it does not define who Johnny can become, but it does give some information about who he is. It is less okay to say, "Johnny is artistic." It is better to say, "Johnny has artistic ability." It is not okay to say, "Johnny is the artist in the family." That not only puts undue pressure on Johnny, it may also limit what Susy thinks about herself.

State facts clearly.

When you describe or introduce your child, begin with intransitive verbs and statements which are undeniable and verifiable fact. "Johnny is our third son, the fourth born." "Susy is our seven-

Principles of Learning

year-old red-headed girl." "Bobby is working through the 3rd grade." "Lucy is involved in 4-H." "Madeline is interested in art."

Describe achievements.

Continue by using transitive (action) verbs that describe current events or recent accomplishments. "Alice made a cake by herself yesterday. She enjoys needle crafts and working with young children." "Rick recently enrolled in a course to learn computer skills and plans to earn a degree in computer science." "Tony learned to add last week. He is building a model car." These statements are just as descriptive, don't limit who the child is, encourage them to be involved in doing, yet don't discourage their siblings.

End the description with a statement about the child's character and your pride or joy in him.

Hold character up.

"It has been a joy to watch Elizabeth gaining self-control. She is working so hard!" "Mike's dad and I are really proud of the way he is developing diligence and patience." "We love to see the way Tom strives to express his love and concern in active ways." "It is exciting to see Brenda growing in graciousness and wisdom." This gives them gentle direction and something to strive to become. At the same time it confirms the positive strides you want to see continued and lets them know that you notice and appreciate their efforts.

45

⇨ Timeless Teaching Tips

Make it a habit.

Now the trick is to actually change a deeply ingrained habit. The first step in changing any habit is to become aware of the need to change and an alternative for which to strive. We've just done that. The next step is to start doing things differently. Take some time soon to sit down and write out a description of each of your children following the formula just given. Make it a long description with several examples. Do your thinking in this unpressured situation. List as many intransitive descriptions (objective indisputable facts) as you can think of for each child. Name at least five things each child is currently involved in or has recently completed. Think hard to find ways your children are growing in character qualities which they will need to be the godly adults you are striving to raise. Make a list of character qualities you want to encourage and have them foremost in your mind as you observe your family daily. Be looking for positive things to comment on. Take notes, because our minds come equipped with great forgetters!

Practice in private.

You may find it easier to write a description of one child each week until you have completed each member of the family. Post these descriptions where you will see them frequently for a while -- perhaps inside your closet door or on your bathroom mirror. Reread them aloud every day for a week to keep the ideas fresh in your mind and to begin hearing yourself talk in this new way. Write a letter to someone who lives far away and

Principles of Learning

describe each of your children without looking at your notes. Confide in a friend or your spouse as to what you are doing and ask if you can practice describing the children to them. Ask if they have any ideas that could be added.

Then be brave! Try it out the next time you have the opportunity to describe or introduce one of your children. Do it whenever possible in their hearing. They will be encouraged!

Habits are made -- or broken -- a little at a time. Don't be discouraged if you slip back into the old way. Just catch yourself as soon as possible

Step by Step

and think about why you are making the change. Watch when you say, "John **is**..." Try to follow that little word is with something that is indisputable. It is all right to describe our children, but we don't want to cast them into an uncomfortable mold. We don't want them living in the shadow of our definition. Be positive. Give your child a reputation to live up to, not one that drags him down. We all have a tendency to perform as others expect. Allow this tendency to work for you and the future of your children.

 **Timeless Teaching Tips**

Increasing Creativity

Every person has some creativity because we were made in the image of the Creator.

In His Image

We all think differently, hold different things as most important, and see different sides of issues. This is perfectly within God's plan because He has different work for each of us to do. Many people do not consider themselves to be creative yet wish to encourage the development of creativity in their children. Creativity can be multiplied through exercise. Here are some ways to stretch the creativity of your children.

Study the world or some small category of it, such as plants, rocks, or soils. Marvel at the vast number of different things in each category and

Study God's World

the number of categories of things that exist without assistance or intervention of man. Take note of the things every (person, dog, tree, flower, etc.) have in common that make them what they are, yet the many variations that make each one different from all others. We all know what a person is and have no trouble at all differentiating a person from a tree, a dog, or a monkey. Try describing how one is different from the other.

Principles of Learning

Then choose one aspect of each. Begin to look at noses, or eyes, or faces. Note that all are basically the same yet all are uniquely different. This activity will greatly increase your understanding of the many facets of each thing which can be studied, compared, and contrasted. Try your hand at drawing different leaves, noses, or eyes. Show with your pencil how they are different. This will help you see variations. Then find words to tell about the differences.

All children are born with creativity. They are born curious and interested in the world around them.

You are creative!

Various responses in their world shape their willingness to express this creativity - and their ability to increase it. Become alert to ways to stretch the creativity of your children. Learn to stop saying "You can't." Allow them to try. They will learn far more from the attempt, even if they fail, than they can if they never are allowed to try. In fact, they may accomplish the seemingly impossible. This is not to say put no limits on your children. I believe we are to put moral limits. Parents, however, tend to put many other limits. "There isn't time. We don't have money. You aren't big (short, small, smart, tall, skilled, creative) enough." We put limits that prevent the children from discovering not only their limits, but their potential. They easily develop the "I can't..." attitude. We need to think of ability, not disability!

Find time!

Time for creativity stretchers can be discovered in easily wasted minutes: waiting for a train, dinner to be ready, or daddy to come home. Many take nothing more than speaking and thinking and no more preparation than thinking yourself.

⇨ Timeless Teaching Tips

Try some of these open-ended statements to fill up the empty minutes:

• Name all the (round things, animals, colors, books, etc. etc.) you can.

• Think of all the ways you could get from _____ to _____.

• How are _____ and _____ alike? How are they different?
a comb and a brush
a box and a bag
a dog and a squirrel
a wall and a floor
a typewriter and a computer   a hand and a foot
a book and a magazine
a pen and a pencil
a clock and a calendar
paper and cloth

How could you use _____ to teach _____?
popcorn, math
clay, history
eggs, science   scissors, language
peanut butter, humility   business cards, nobility

Get your students to think about characteristics, relationship, similarities, and differences. Give them many experiences and encourage them to compare, describe, and evaluate. Get busy and develop their creativity and you may find your own increasing as well!

Principles of Learning

Learning Within the Family

Goals and Goal Setting

Many families feel they just bounce around and never accomplish anything. The first step toward a solution is recognizing that

What is the problem?

there is a problem. Next it helps to verbalize just what the need is. What do you hope to accomplish? What do you want your children to learn? What do you hope to have finished in the next (week, year, decade)? At that point it may be beneficial to write down possible solutions. Be free. Brain storm without judging at first so the ideas flow freely. Then think of pros and cons of each idea. Select the best. Try something. If it doesn't work, don't be at all discouraged. You have just found one thing that doesn't work. That narrows the field! The real answer may be just around the corner.

Help me see progress.

One of the best motivators toward accomplishing some-thing is to see evidence of your progress. It is impossible to see

51

➡ Timeless Teaching Tips

progress unless you set achievable and measurable goals. Not every skill can be charted, but it is important to chart some goals in order to see movement. Without such goals, it is more likely that learning will be unfocused and unrecognized. That often leads to feeling stalled and ineffective.

Some structure is needed both in life and in school. That doesn't mean (if you are homeschooling) bringing school home. On the contrary, that much formal structure may be constrictive or even in many situations, counterproductive. It's better to just set some long term and short term goals.

In the academic areas, get a scope and sequence from a reputable curriculum publisher. This is a list of skills or concepts covered, usually grade level by grade level, listed in order presented. It is available at no cost from most curriculum publishers. World Book Encyclopedia also publishes one. There are also books which give an idea of what can be taught at each grade level - or what must be covered in the elementary grades, middle school ages and high schools. Remember, children differ. Use these as guides, not as a god. Though I personally resist too much restriction by age and grade level, I have written both a mini-book on *SIMPLIFIED Homeschool and Recordkeeping* which contains a general scope and sequence for kindergarten through sixth grade and also a full list of academic skills from kindergarten through the eighth grade called *Luke's School List*. There is also a companion of spiritual, character and life skills called *Luke's Life List*. Use one or more of these as your guide to choose some topics to approach in the next few months.

Principles of Learning

It is not always possible to determine ahead how long it will take to cover a topic or to learn a skill, but it is helpful to have a developmental sequence to give you an idea where you are going. This also makes it possible to be gathering materials for future studies when you notice them. Keep a drawer or a file cabinet ready to organize these finds so they'll be ready when you are. Keep note also of library books which address the topic, questions that come up that you'll want to research, and articles you come across in magazines or on the internet. Jot down ideas for possible field trips. I find that sometimes under pressure, these ideas remain hidden in the vast recesses of my brain, but when I at last need them they are jumping out and ready for use. Keep future topics in mind and jot down the ideas as you find them and file them immediately. They will start you thinking in the right direction long before deadlines threaten.

It is also helpful to involve the children in goal setting. Ask their opinion when choosing topics, methods of study, and the manner of showing effort and progress. Be willing to compromise where possible, but remember that you are ultimately the one held responsible for their education.

In a given study, make a list of skills to be mastered, facts to be memorized, jobs to be done, or books to be read. Turn the list into a chart ready to date, mark off, or award a sticker when the job is done or the skill is mastered. Seeing the chart fill up is very rewarding and keeps efforts directed. Do allow diversions when they are important; just add them to the chart so you can still see progress and direction. The important thing here is to structure a way to document accomplishments.

Chart What Is to be Learned

⇨ Timeless Teaching Tips

Record Level of Development

Another way to see progress is to have the children make an informal record of their present level of development, and repeat the same activity every three to six months. I often had my students list ten words they could spell, write a story or paragraph and make up and solve one problem for each aspect of math they were familiar with (addition, subtraction, decimals, money, fractions, etc.). This gave me a running record of their handwriting, spelling, and math and, indirectly, their reading level as well. Perhaps a better evaluation of their reading would be to have them list three of the best books they have read since the last time they did this. **Be sure they put their name and date on this paper!** Keep them in sequential order, most recent on top, in a section of the child's portfolio and refer to them occasionally. You will be amazed at how easy it is to see maturation and skill in this simple way.

Take photos!

Some progress can be best recorded through taking photos. Photograph large projects, presentations, and field trips. Then have the children enter the photos in an album and add captions. These will be great for record-keeping, reminiscing and sharing with interested friends and relatives. Writing captions provides meaningful practice of handwriting, improves spelling, and teaches the formulation of thoughts into sentences and paragraphs. And it's more fun that an assignment for the sake of an assignment.

Post Goals

Setting goals and posting them in front of you keeps you directed and goal oriented. I find sticky notes invaluable

Principles of Learning

for keeping current goals in the front of my mind. I love to write "DONE" on top of goals, and even enjoy discarding the stickies when I complete all the tasks on them. You might prefer to date the stickies and keep them in your child's portfolio. Whatever way you choose, the key is to keep goals in the front of your mind so that they do not become neglected and forgotten before they are finished. No one finishes everything he starts, but you can always make improvements by setting goals, keeping them in front of you, and charting progress on a regular basis.

 **Timeless Teaching Tips**

Do: Involve: Explain

Learning takes place in comfortable and homey settings. There are some things which are better taught in a structured and sequential way, at least to some children. On the other hand, many things are caught and not taught. There is a simple formula for success. Do. Involve. Explain.

Whatever you do, involve your children. Explain as you go what you are doing and why.

I learned this from Tom, my husband. He does this all the time. It's amazing. The neighborhood children love to come over. They come over and ask, "Can Mr. Tom come out and play?" He thinks of something he needs to do (usually outdoors) and lets them tag along. He talks to them about what he is doing and answers their questions. If they wander off, as long as they are in sight and not hurting anything, he leaves them alone. Often they wander back for more.

Principles of Learning

Show and Tell

Sometimes he gets out a harmonica or keyboard, or his set of bells. He shows them and tells them what he is doing. Pretty soon, he is pointing to the right bell or key and the child is instantly playing a recognizable song. The next time they come, he may not have time to spend with them. Then he just gets out one instrument and lets them experiment on their own. They still love it!

What do You Have?

Some days he looks at something we have and then he finds a way to entertain them with it. One day he had two of them put their hands on our copy machine. He left the lid up and copied their hands. Then he labeled each hand with the child's name and date and sent it home to their family. They were back later with two siblings for the same treatment!

Another time he took a group for a walk. They talked and he answered their questions. It was a rare time of closeness for those children. It is in those infrequent times of "nothing to do" that people open up and become themselves. As they walked, one child asked, "Why do people do the horrible things we see on the news?" He responded quietly, "People naturally do bad things. That is easy. We need God's help to do what is right. Do you want God to help you do what is right?" That little trip ended with his having the opportunity to share salvation with them.

You may wonder how we get anything done. Well, basically we have made only one rule: once a day. Between their short

➡ Timeless Teaching Tips

attention spans and their mom calling them away, we rarely have to ask them to leave.

When working with your own family, this is best instituted when the children are small. Two-year-olds want to follow. They copy everything they see. They are full of interest. They want to learn. By the time they are twelve or thirteen, if you have never involved them before, they are likely to have developed their own world. This is not as likely to have happened with home schooling, but even there we can become so focused on "educating" our children that we neglect to develop a relationship with them. What a tragedy!

Children Are People!

Children are people first. They have feelings and needs and longings. And, even more important, they have spiritual needs. It takes time together doing "nothing" to earn the privilege of sharing their innermost thoughts. Take a lesson from my husband: build into your schedule informal times to be together and get to know your kids.

Principles of Learning

Principles of Changing Behavior

"**Pick it up!** Right Now! Did you hear me? Why aren't you doing it? If you don't pick it up right now, you'll be sorry! Did you hear what I said? All Right. That's it! One...Two..."

Sound familiar? In homes across our country scenes like this are being played out every day. Children and parents are constantly at odds. Children are challenging their parents' authority. We expect that from two-year-olds and teenagers! But we do expect that there will be a few years in between where living together is the joy it was meant to be - or at least a few minutes! What happened to picnics at the lake, trips to the museum, and looking at constellations on a clear summer evening? Who cares any more? It's hard enough to get the basics done - like earning a living, keeping the house in order, and seeing that the kids have clean clothes and don't kill each other. There's not time enough in the day to find a minute to gather your thoughts, sigh in relief, put your feet up, or consider what type of music you'd like to listen to. And all against a background of constant quibbling, arguing, or even downright yelling and fighting. That will quickly suck enthusiasm and love out of life. It doesn't have to be that

⇨ Timeless Teaching Tips

way. In many of these situations there are ways to circumvent confrontations and prevent or avoid the seemingly inevitable blow up. Frequently it is a matter of taking control, communicating that control and recognizing some of your children's' basic needs when planning and making decisions.

> **Communication is essential.**

Communication between the two parents is truly essential. Communication with the children being disciplined is equally important. Both parents must jointly agree on which behaviors will be acceptable, which behaviors will be not be tolerated, what discipline or punishment is appropriate and where and when it will be administered. First parents must communicate with each other to set the tone and establish priorities. Later they will need to communicate the ground rules to the children. This takes time and may need to be done gradually and in stages. The first step should begin before there are children - or even before there is a marriage. If a couple discovers huge differences of opinion on how to approach this topic, there may be other major differences as well. This may be catastrophic or beneficial, depending upon how it is perceived. Let me give you an example.

I recently met a couple who were in constant conflict with and regarding one of their children. Their daughter was not quite seven and very demanding, hyperactive, boisterous, rebellious, and defiant. Learning was progressing very slowly, outings were becoming a trial, and the family was being torn apart. As we talked, the truth gradually surfaced. We compared rules and discipline to being fences that define the boundaries of approved

Principles of Learning

behavior. The dad admitted that he grew up with no fences at all. He knew that was not healthy and was determined that his family would know **exactly** where the fence was. Rules would be tight. Discipline would be strict. Punishment would be immediate and forceful. His children would not be raised in the loose and amoral way he had grown up. Mom, on the other hand, said her background was very different. Her mother didn't have just a fence. She had a "concrete wall with daggers coming out of the top!"

Each was reacting against the way they had been raised by going to the opposite extreme. Both sensed that their spouse was "exactly like my mom." So each spouse moved further in the opposite direction. Conflict was constant. A very bright and creative child was caught in between the parents and their past. Though she appeared to be very unreasonable and obnoxious, she was reacting in very normal ways against the confusing and conflicting demands being made on her. God had put into their home the very child needed to sand off their rough edges. The real problem was that both parents were reacting to the sandpaper instead of submitting to the Master.

The first problem here was a lack of communication. Each child needs to know and understand his limits. This Mom and Dad had

Teach me my limits.

never agreed on a game plan appropriate for their present family. Each was independently rebelling against the extremes under which he had been raised and unknowingly recreating the spouse's paternal family. Each was also feeling that the other was unreasonably like his own parents and definitely in the

➡ Timeless Teaching Tips

wrong. Just getting that out into the open went a long way toward finding the solution. In reality each had the right ingredients for keeping their spouse from becoming extreme. As they realized this, they were able to find the narrow, but healthy, road to happiness.

As one parent says, "I think it should be this way," the other may respond, "No, that didn't work in my family. Let's try ___" The important part of this step is to **really** be open to hear the negative side of what you, as a child, thought would be the perfect way to be raised. These parents needed to communicate to discover that neither laisse faire nor blind autocracy created the results they were looking for. Finally the parents were able to see that either extreme was harmful and took steps toward a more reasonable middle path. After agreeing on the tone of discipline and punishment the next stage was to list specific rules for their family and determine how these would be communicated and carried out.

> **To know the rules gives me warm security and helps me understand God's love.**

In many families, schools, work places, churches, rules are never stated clearly. Sometimes both the rules and the way they are enforced differs depending on which person is in control at the moment. Both approaches give all of us, but children in particular, a feeling of insecurity and lack of control. It feels to them like walking on a surface of jello. They're never sure how sturdy it is or when they will slip up and get hurt. They **need** to know that there is a boundary and that there is something or someone stronger than they - someone who can

Principles of Learning

set reasonable limits and then keep them within the limits. I believe this is crucial to their understanding a loving but firm God. If they find no one capable of making and enforcing rules while they are small, they have difficulty as adults understanding that there is any God or government who has the power or the right to make limits on their behavior.

Both parents need to agree on what rules they are willing to enforce. Rules should be stated as clearly as possible. The consequence of breaking the rule should be made clear as well. Whenever possible this should be a natural consequence such as, "If you are not dressed properly when we are ready to leave you may not go with us." For younger children, a poster with pictures or symbols of appropriate behaviors may be helpful. Don't have more rules than you both are willing to enforce. Don't try to establish a host of rules all at once. Multiple instructions create multiple confusion.

Enforce the rules you make.

Following are some possible and reasonable family rules stated in positive terms.

Our Family Rules

• Our family will show respect for each other and for other people and their things.

• Our family will speak calmly and try to carefully explain their feelings.

Timeless Teaching Tips

•Our family will respect, honor and worship God through all relationships.

•Children in our family will be in bed by 9 PM, unless the parents agree on extenuating circumstances

I have seen families with too few rules and families with too many rules. In essence, the fewer, the better. God initially presented Ten Commandments. Jesus shortened that to two, and then added the "Golden Rule." There are two "universal laws" which are also helpful: "Do what you say you'll do," and "Don't hurt anyone." There is only one Biblical rule specifically directed toward children: "Children, obey your parents."

Stating rules in positive terms helps children desire to work with them rather than rebel against them. Stating them in terms of "our family will..." gives ammunition against "but everybody else is..." when it surfaces. When possible, let the children have a voice in determining family rules. Reserve the right of veto, but use it as sparingly as possible. Consult the Scriptures for guidance.

Knowing and communicating what the rules are is not enough. **Children have a need to feel some control.** This is particularly true of children who are very bright, have potential leadership ability or are strong-willed. This is not a want or stubbornness; it is a need! It is also an important step toward maturing and gaining a sense of responsibility. The trick

Principles of Learning

is, in the younger years especially, for the parents to maintain basic control (a need of the child) and yet to allow the children to have some control (another real need of the child). Usually this can be accomplished through what I have come to call "shared control."

Shared control is giving the child a choice within a framework set by the adult. Here are some examples:

- "We're going to write. Would you like to write on the chalkboard or on paper?" When he responds, go on: "What color (paper, chalk) would you like to use?"

- "It's almost bedtime. Would you like to go to bed in ten minutes and cuddle with a book for ten minutes or play a little longer and go to bed in twenty minutes?" (Offer this option only after they are dressed and **ready** for bed.)

- "It's time for school. Would you like to do math or spelling first?"

- "It's time for spelling. Would you like to write the word or spell it out loud?"

- "I need to have something to show that you read and studied that chapter. Would you like to answer the questions at the end, outline the chapter, or list ten important ideas and highlight the three most important ones?"

- "You need to do a book report on _____. Would you like to write it, give it orally, or do a project?" If they choose orally, tape record it and include it in their portfolio. If they do a

⇨ Timeless Teaching Tips

project, take a snapshot of them with the finished result, date it and include it in their portfolio.

> **Set the outer limit. Allow a choice.**

The adult sets the outer limit. Make the first statement calmly and without wavering. Do not follow it with, "Okay?" or say it with any hesitancy. The parent is definitely in control, but the needs, personality and desires of the child should be considered. This approach lessens tension, gives both feelings of being in control, and smoothes the path to actually accomplishing something, while it builds a bridge between the parent and child. The child senses that the parent cares about his feelings and who he is. The parent sees the child begin to take responsibility for his decisions. Each will be bonded to the other.

There are times when the parent can offer no choice. Some rules must be enforced rigidly. Keep these as few as possible, and even then try to offer a choice: "Would you like to do that now, or after discipline?"

> **Eliminate power struggles!**

Offering limited choices is a way of sharing control and saving face. It eliminates the power struggles that are common when dealing with children. It is freeing - both to the adult and to the child. Now you have the information. Put it into practice as soon as possible! Would you like to start with your son, your daughter, or your spouse?

Principles of Learning

What about Commitment, Respect, and Obedience?

Why aren't kids today learning to make commitments... to respect authority... to persevere... to obey? We learn most lessons by observing the people closest to us day after day in good times and in bad. We obey because we respect. We respect because we love. We love because we have been loved. We make commitments because someone in our lives has been committed to us.

Today's society is transient. Mom and Dad work. The kids shuffle from school to after-school-care to bed and back again. No one has the time to enjoy a falling snowflake or to watch a flower bloom. Television happens in twenty-second segments presenting a problem and solving it within a twenty-minute time period dotted with thirty-second commercials. We eat fast foods, cook instant potatoes and cereal, and expect to dash through the line at the bank, the discount store or the

⇨ Timeless Teaching Tips

supermarket. Workbook pages require instant answers. Everything happens on the run.

Take time to make a difference.

Decide to take the time to make a difference in the lives of your children. Don't look at them as objects to be owned or subjects to be educated. Tackle a project that will take time and consistent commitment. Build a dollhouse, add a room on the house, make a quilt, or create a canoe from a kit. Do it together! Let every member be in on it from beginning planning stages to the final joy of completion. Take pictures of the steps and date them. When you are enjoying the final project, look at the pictures and remind yourselves of the hard work, the amount of time required to created this and the fun you had working together. Enjoy the feelings of accomplishing a difficult task. Then begin planning the next project.

Principles of Learning

Scared by a Two Year Old

Something happened to me the other day that really scared me.

My husband and I were meeting another couple for breakfast and we arrived first. I went in to hold a table. At a nearby booth a small child - about two years old - was seated in a booster chair. She was alone. Only a stack of napkins and silver on the other side of the booth indicated that someone might be coming back to her. She seemed very vulnerable in our unpredictable world, but that is not what scared me.

I didn't get scared until her mother came.

The child was alone for close to five minutes. She was cheerful and contented, nibbling away at her healthy, well-balanced meal. Then her mother came with her own plate of food. She didn't sit down, but spoke to her daughter.

"Would you like for me to sit here, or there next to you?" After getting no visible or audible response, the mother repeated her question more forcefully. "Would you like for me to sit across from you, or right there beside you?"

➩ Timeless Teaching Tips

The child looked at her mother and continued to eat. Finally the mother asked, "Do you hear me?"

"I can't answer right now." The child spoke clearly and succinctly.

"Why not?" her mother questioned. The child popped a piece of bacon into her mouth and said, "Because I am eating."

It was thoughtful of the mother to ask whether the child preferred for her to sit next to or across from her - once. It was careless of her to continue this conversation which obviously did not interest her daughter at all. But it was downright frightening that she gave this child so much power over her own life. (And I'm not even dealing with the rudeness of the daughter. That was also ignored.)

Everywhere I go I see parents who are busy trying to please their infants, toddlers and preschoolers. Some of them are still waiting on and consulting their school-age children. Most of them, by the time they have school-age children, are frustrated, exhausted and about ready to pull their hair out! And their children are rude, crude, thoughtless, lazy and unreasonably irritable.

What went wrong?

The sad thing is they can't figure out what went wrong. They adored their precious, sweet little infant. They loved their cute precocious toddler. They tolerated their

Principles of Learning

brash, busy preschooler thinking it was a stage he would grow out of. Now they don't even like their obnoxious child. They are blind to the fact that they are merely living with the consequences of their own actions.

This scenario reminds me of a situation some neighbors of mine once found themselves in. They had gotten a St. Bernard puppy. It was so cute and cuddly. It loved to run and play and they soon trained it to do many tricks. One of the tricks was signaled by their standing with their legs slightly separated. The puppy ran between their legs. It was so cute! Cute that is until the puppy was an adult. Anytime anyone stood with their legs slightly spread, the dog took off tearing through. Many unprepared people were suddenly toppled to the ground. It wasn't cute anymore; but how to you teach the dog that he is too big now to do what was so cute when he was a puppy?

Children are naturally followers. They want to learn. They want to please their parents. When we expect them to lead us and spend our lives trying to please them, we reverse the rolls that God designed. It may appear cute at first, but it can only be headed for disaster.

We are still reacting, I'm afraid, to our aversion to the autocratic, no-nonsense, children-are-to-be-seen-and-not-heard stories that we heard about past generations. We seem to have three generations or so that continue to react to the "Life With Father" militarism of the late 1800's. Now we've turned to a new century. The pendulum has shifted about as far as it can. Is it possible for this generation of parents to respond carefully and thoughtfully rather than reacting? Is it possible for today's parents and would-be parents to consider the scriptures and

⇨ Timeless Teaching Tips

"train up a child in the way he should go?" Will this generation diligently teach their children to obey God by talking His words when they sit in their house, while they walk by the way, and when they lie down and rise up? Will you?

Principles of Learning

Grandma Scares Me, Too

There we were sitting in another restaurant watching another family on an average day of the year. The whole family was there: mom, dad, two children and grandma. Grandma was pretty busy keeping a careful eye on the two-year-old. (Good for her; nobody else was.) The four-year-old looked over and spoke to her, "Shame on you, Grandma! You shouldn't have done that. You were naughty!"

Nothing had happened that I saw. It was out of the blue. Obviously it referred to something they both knew about, though, for Grandma's response was, "Yes, I was naughty."

"Good for her," I thought - until her next phrase summed it all up: "That's just how I am."

In that one phrase so quickly given, she gave her granddaughter tacit approval to never accept responsibility for anything - failure, leaving a task undone, bad attitude, sin... after all she, too, could always say, "That's just how I am."

➪ Timeless Teaching Tips

When will we learn that we teach more by how we handle things - by those little comments that slip by so easily - by our own attitude toward sin and failure - than we could preach in a year of one-hour-daily lectures?

We aren't responsible for much in this world. Only our every:
WORD
THOUGHT
ACTION
ATTITUDE
MOTIVE

Oh, my, that is everything! All the time! Even a careless word quickly given in a restaurant!

We are responsible for what we do with every thought that comes into our mind. We are responsible for every attitude and motive which we allow to form in our heart. We are responsible for every word and deed that comes out in our lives. That is awesome responsibility which far too many of us take casually - even carelessly.

There is a solution. There are things we can do to turn around those careless words.

First of all, we must really **clarify our worldview** - the underlying beliefs upon which we base everything we say and do and think. Many of us were raised in a secular public school. Many of us had worldly, unchurched

Principles of Learning

parents. Many of our underlying motives were formed when we were two and four-years-old by off-hand comments of our parents and grandparents. We don't have to go back and rake our past and our parents through the coals, but we do have to examine what is truth. Until we do, we'll not even notice when we pass along the world's lies. Topics we must consider are: God, Man, the World, Authority, Truth, Values, and Ethics. The Bible is the first source, of course. There are many others. Two of my favorites are Dr. Francis Schaeffer's *How Should We Then Live?* and *Why So Many Christians Are Going Home To School* by Ellyn Davis.

Limit the ungodly influences which enter our homes through television, toys, magazines, and heroes of passion and strength. Take a look around your home. What do you see? Look at the walls, the floors, the table tops, even the closets. What your children see day after day influences them more than many of your words.  Have you posted the Ten Commandments? Are the pictures on the wall reflective of God and His love and creation? Are the books and magazines godly examples of right living? Are the clothes you wear and those you provide for your children modest and appropriate for Kingdom children? What about the toys? Do they lead your children to godly thoughts and healthy imitative play?

One lady was asking her pastor, "Why did all my boys go out to sea? I've missed so much of their lives. I just don't understand." He replied, "I do. Look." He pointed

⇨ Timeless Teaching Tips

to a picture on the wall - a sailing vessel riding the waves. The boys had seen that picture daily in their childhood and it had become part of them. They had modeled their lives after what they had seen day after day.

One year when I was teaching in a Christian school, our class decided to exchange gifts at Christmas. To ensure that no child went home empty-handed, I went to the toy department and bought a couple of gifts to keep on hand. One was a cute little car which, with a few deft twists, could be transformed into a robot. I was glad I had that on hand. When one boy came without anything to share, I gave the car/robot. Later that afternoon the child returned it to me. He didn't want to keep it. Puzzled, I asked why. He showed me the robot. It had a very small, very evil face. Then he pointed to the packaging. In tiny, tiny words it said "Evil Deceiver." Fortunately, the toy had gone to an observant boy with a very sensitive spirit. The marketers for toys are especially deceptive. Be wary!

I can't emphasize too much the influence of the things your children see and hear every day. We teach far more than our lesson plans reveal. Children are deeply impressed by casual interactions with the adults in their lives. Do they ever catch you on your knees? Do they see that the Bible is an important part of your day? Do they hear love and encouragement pouring from your lips? Do they bask in an atmosphere of inspiration and joy? Do they ever hear you admit fault and ask forgiveness? Do you speak the truth in big and little issues? Or are you telling them to do right and showing them to do wrong?

Principles of Learning

We must bathe our relationships in the Word of God. What goes in will come out. Give yourself and those in your life happy, cheerful, warm and wonderful experiences with God's Word.

Bathe in God's Word.

Read the Bible out loud in unison. Take parts and read it like a play. Read an important passage daily until you can recite it. Discuss how it has changed your life. Listen to audio presentations which have added sound effects to make the Word come alive. There are even a few video presentations which are Scripturally accurate and make the Bible come alive for visual learners.

Younger children love to act out the stories of the Word. Make sure they are taught the principles and lessons - not just the events. Provide them with

Act out the Word

costumes and help them with props. The teens in our small church created a television news program interviewing the characters from the book of Esther. They video-taped it and also performed it live for the church. They are excited about the Word! They are living the words and thoughts of godliness.

I used to act in a community theater. I had to give it up. I noticed that when I lived the part for week after week in rehearsals, it became a part of me - and the parts got more and more worldly and less and less exemplary. Acting out the lives of biblical characters, missionaries, preachers, and other morally sound people of the past will cement in your children's lives many of the principles you are seeking to instill.

⇨ Timeless Teaching Tips

Lay it all on the altar.

Lay your past, your present and the future on the altar and ask for God's blessing and guidance - and His healing and cleansing. Ask Him to reveal anything which needs to be cleansed from your life. Offer Him a sensitive, receptive heart, a willingness to serve, and a life cleansed or ready-to-clean. Remember, He is the Launderer of the Heart. We cannot rid ourselves of every thought, but with His help, we can fill our minds so full with truth and love and joy that there is no room for evil to take root. We cannot behave perfectly in our families or in restaurants - but we can ask God to reveal the truth behind our words and attitudes. We cannot control everything in our lives, but we can pray for wisdom and ask God to guide us and make us more aware - and to protect our little ones.

We cannot do everything, but we can do something. We will make mistakes. We will fail; but we can only succeed if we continue to try.

It's Been Said

👓 👓 👓 👓 👓 👓 👓 👓

Introduction	79
Education	81
America as A Nation	82
Science	92
Worldview	94
God and The Bible	95
Important Quotes of Famous People	97

It's Been Said 👓

It's Been Said...

Introduction

"All that is necessary for evil to triumph is for good men to do nothing."
Edmund Burke (1729-1797)
British Statesman

"...The genuine source of correct republican principles is the Bible, particularly the New Testament or the Christian religion."
Noah Webster (1758-1843)
educator and journalist
American Dictionary of the English Language

"Upon my arrival in the United States, the religious aspects of the country was the first thing that struck my attention; and the longer I stayed there, the more did I perceive the great political consequences resulting from this state of things, to which I was unaccustomed. In France I had almost always seen the spirit of religion and the spirit of freedom pursuing courses diametrically

➪ Timeless Teaching Tips

opposed to each other; but in America I found that they were truly united, and that they reigned in common over the same country."
Alexis de Tocqueville (1805-1859)
French Historian and Philosopher

"Instead of the ill-advised hopes of the last two centuries, which have reduced us to insignificance and brought us to the brink of nuclear and non-nuclear death, we can only reach with determination for the warm hand of God, which we have so rashly and self-confidently pushed away."
Alexander Solzhenitsyn (1918-   )
Russian Novelist, won Nobel Prize for literature

"I believe that the next half century will determine if we will advance the cause of Christian civilization or revert to the horrors of brutal paganism."
President Theodore Roosevelt (1858-1919)
26th President of the United States of America 1901-1929

It's Been Said 👓

Education

"Education is useless without the Bible."
Noah Webster (1758-1843)
American Educator and Journalist - Webster's Dictionary

"Let every Student be plainly instructed, and earnestly pressed to consider well, the main end of his life and studies is, to know God and Jesus Christ which is eternall life."
Harvard University, 1642, Rules and Precepts

"Cursed be all learning that is contrary to the cross of Christ."
Jonathan Dickinson, First President of Princeton University

"Just as eating against one's will is injurious to health, so study without a liking for it spoils the memory, and it retains nothing it takes in."
Leonardo Da Vinci (1452-1519)
Great Artist and Thinker

"A thorough knowledge of the Bible is worth more than a college education."
Theodore Roosevelt (1858-1919)
26th President of the United States (1901-1909)

"I have alternately been called an Aristocrat and a Democrat. I am neither. I am a Christocrat."
Dr. Benjamin Rush
"Father of the Public Schools"
Signer of the Declaration of Independence

"The Congress of the United States approves and recommends to the people, the Holy Bible...for use in schools."
Congress of the United States 1781

 **Timeless Teaching Tips**

America as a Nation

"It cannot be emphasized too strongly or too often that this great nation was founded, not by religionists, but by Christians; not on religions, but on the gospel of Jesus Christ! For this very reason people of other faiths have been afforded asylums, prosperity and freedom of worship here."

Patrick Henry (1736-1799)
Distinguished American Statesman

"If we ever forget that we are One Nation Under God, then we will be a Nation gone under."

Ronald Reagan (1911-)
40th President of the United States (1981-1989)

"Our laws and our institutions must necessarily be based upon and embody the teachings of the Redeemer of mankind. It is impossible that it should be otherwise; and in this sense and to this extent our civilization and our institutions are emphatically Christian. "

United States Supreme Court 1892
Church of the Holy Trinity vs. United States

It's Been Said 👓

"All must admit that the reception of the teachings of Christ results in the purest patriotism, in the most scrupulous fidelity to public trust, and in the best type of citizenship. "
Grover Cleveland (1837-1908)
22nd President of the United States (1855-1889, 1893-1987)

"In ye name of God, Amen. We whose names are underwriten, the loyal subjects of our dread soveraigne Lord, King James, by ye grace of God..."
The Pilgrim's Mayflower Compact 11-11-1620

"The fear of God is the beginning of wisdom and its consummation is everlasting felicity."
William Samuel Johnson , Signer of the Constitution, Political & Educational Leader

"A more beautiful or precious morsel of ethics I have never seen; it is a document in proof that I am a real Christian; that is to say, a disciple of the doctrines of Jesus."
Thomas Jefferson (1743-1826)
3rd President of the United States (1801-1809)

"To the distinguished character of Patriot, it should be our highest Glory to laud the more distinguished Character of Christian."
General George Washington (1736-1789)
First President of the United States 1789-1797)
Father of Our Country

"I am apt to believe that it will be celebrated by succeeding generations as the great anniversary Festival. It ought to be commemorated, as the day of deliverance, by solemn acts of devotion to God Almighty."
John Adams
2nd President of the United States (1797-1801)
written to his wife Abigail on the day following the approval by Congress of the Declaration of Independence

⇨ Timeless Teaching Tips

"We have staked the future of all of our political institutions upon the capacity of mankind for self-government; upon the capacity of each and all of us to govern ourselves, to control ourselves, to sustain ourselves according to the Ten Commandments of God."
James Madison (1751-1836)
4th President of the United States (1809-1817)

"The fundamental basis of this nation's laws was given to Moses on the Mount."
Harry S.Truman (1884-1972)
33rd President of the Unites States (1945-1953)

"We are a Christian people... According to one another the equal right of religious freedom, and acknowledge with reverence the duty of obedience to the will of God."
United States Supreme Court, 1939
case of Hague vs. C. I. O.

"Religion, morality, and knowledge [are] necessary to good government, the preservation of liberty, and the happiness of mankind"
United States Supreme Court, 1925
case of Pierce v. Society of Sisters

"It is impossible to rightly govern the world without God and the Bible."
George Washington (1732-1799)

"The general principles on which the fathers achieved independence were... the general principles of Christianity."
John Adams (1735-1826)

"God grant that in America true religion and civil liberty may be inseparable. ...He is the best friend to American liberty who is most sincere and active in promoting true and undefiled religion."
John Witherspoon (1723-1794)
Signer of **Declaration of Independence**

It's Been Said 👓

"Providence (God) has given to our people the choice of their rulers and it is the duty as well as the privilege and interest of our Christian nation to select and prefer Christians for their rulers"
John Jay (1745-1829)
1ˢᵗ Chief Justice - negotiated treaty of peace to end Revolutionary War

"We have all been encouraged to feel in the guardianship and guidance of that Almighty Being whose power regulates the destiny of nations..."
James Madison (1751-1836)

"The power to tax involves the power to destroy."
John Marshall (1755-1835)
Great Chief Justice encouraged strong federal government

"Christianity...is not to be maliciously and openly reviled and blasphemed against." He called America a "Christian country."
Joseph Story (1779-1845)
Supreme Court Justice appointed by James Madison

"The highest glory of the American Revolution was this; it connected, in one indissoluble bond, the principles of civil government and the principles of Christianity."
John Quincy Adams (1767-1848)
6ᵗʰ President of the United States
"Old Man Eloquent"

"We are a Christian people, according to one another the equal right of religious freedom and acknowledging with reverence the duty of obedience to the will of God."
1931 - U.S. vs. Macintosh

⇨ Timeless Teaching Tips

"I have lived, Sir, a long time, and the longer I live, the more convincing proof I see of the truth - that God governs in the affairs of men. And if a sparrow cannot fall to the ground without His notice, is it probable that an empire can rise without His aid? We have been assured, Sir, in the sacred writings, that 'except the Lord build the House, they labor in vain that build it.' I firmly believe this; and I also believe that without this concurring aid we shall succeed in this political building no better, than the Builders of Babel: We shall be divided by our partial local interests; our projects will be confounded, and we ourselves shall become a reproach and bye word down to future ages. And what is worse, mankind may hereafter from this unfortunate instance, despair of establishing Government by human wisdom and leave it to chance, war and conquest. I therefore beg leave to move - that henceforth prayers imploring the audience of Heaven, and its blessings on our deliberations, be held in this assembly every morning before we proceed to business, and that one or more of the clergy of this city be requested to officiate in that service."

Benjamin Franklin (1706-1790) - American Statesman, Scientist, Inventor, and Author, Spoken at the Constitutional Convention June 28, 1787

"Religion in America... must nevertheless be regarded as the foremost of the political institutions of that country... I do not know whether all the Americans have a sincere faith in their religion, for who can search the human heart? But I am certain that they hold it to be indispensable to the maintenance of republican institutions. This position is not peculiar to a class of citizens or to a party, but it belongs to the whole nation, and to every rank of society... Christianity, therefore, reigns without any obstacle, by universal consent."

Alexis de Tocqueville

"No person who shall deny the being of God, ...or the divine authority of the Old or New Testaments, or who shall hold religious principles incompatible with the freedom and safety of the State, shall be capable of holding any office or place of trust in the civil department within this State."

North Carolina Constitution 1876

It's Been Said 👓

" I believe no one can read the history of our country without realizing the Good Book and the Spirit of the Savior have from the beginning been our guiding geniuses..."
Earl Warren (1891-1974)
Chief Justice of United States Supreme Court (1953-1969)

"The great vital and conservative element in our system is the belief of our people in the pure doctrines and divine truths of the gospel of Jesus Christ."
House Judiciary Report in 1854

"And can the liberties of a nation be thought secure when we have removed their only firm basis, a conviction in the minds of the people that these liberties are of the gift of God? That they are not to be violated but with His wrath? Indeed I tremble for my country when I reflect that God is just, that His justice cannot sleep forever."
Thomas Jefferson

"This is a religious people. This is historically true. From the discovery of this continent to the present hour, there is a single voice making this affirmation... These are not individual sayings, declarations of private persons: they are organic utterances, they speak the voice of the entire people.... These, and many other matters which might be noticed, add a volume of unofficial declarations to the mass of organic utterances that this is a Christian nation."
US Supreme Court
Church of the Holy Trinity vs. US 1892

"We have no government armed with power capable of contending with human passions unbridled by morality and religion ... Our constitution was made only for a moral and religious people. It is wholly inadequate to the government of any other."
John Adams

I know of no way of judging of the future but by the past... we shall not fight our battles alone. There is a just God who presides over the destinies of nations... Why stand we here idle? ... Is life

⇨ Timeless Teaching Tips

so dear, or peace so sweet, as to be purchased at the price of chains and slavery? Forbid it, Almighty God! I know not what course others may take; but as for me, give me liberty, or give me death!

Patrick Henry
American Statesman, Spoken March 28, 1775

There are instances of, I would say, an almost astonishing Providence in our favor; our success has staggered our enemies, and almost given faith to infidels; so we may truly say it is not our own arm which has saved us. The hand of Heaven appears to have led us on...

Samuel Adams (1722-1803)
great American patriot
Delivered to the State House in Philadelphia August 1, 1776

"It is the duty of nations as well as men to own their dependence upon the overruling power of God, to confess their sins and transgressions in humble sorrow yet with assured hope that genuine repentance will lead to mercy and pardon, and to recognize the sublime truth, announced in the Holy Scriptures and proven by all history: that those nations only are blessed whose God is the Lord."

Abraham Lincoln (1809-1865)
16th President of the United States (1861-1865)

"No free government now exists in the world unless where Christianity is acknowledged and is the religion of the country... Its foundations are broad and strong, and deep.... It is the purest system of morality, the firmest auxiliary, and the only stable support of all human laws."

Supreme Court of Pennsylvania
Updegraph vs. The Commonwealth 1824

It's Been Said 👓

"No people can be bound to acknowledge and adore the Invisible Hand which conducts the affairs of men more than those of the United States. Every step by which they have advanced to the character of an independent nation seems to have been distinguished by some token of providential agency ... We ought to be no less persuaded that the propitious smiles of Heaven can never be expected on a Nation that disregards the eternal rules of order and right which Heaven itself has ordained."
George Washington
Inaugural Speech to Congress April 30, 1789

"The Bible... is the one supreme source of revelation of the meaning of life, the nature of God and spiritual nature and need of men. It is the only guide of life which really leads the spirit in the way of peace and salvation. ...America was born a Christian nation. America was born to exemplify that devotion to the elements of righteousness which are derived from the revelations of the Holy Scripture."
Woodrow Wilson (1856-1924)
28th President of the United States (1913-1921)

"The real object of the First Amendment was not to countenance, much less to advance, Mohammedanism, or Judaism, or infidelity, by prostrating Christianity, but to exclude all rivalry among Christian sects, and to prevent any national ecclesiastical establishment which would give to an hierarchy the exclusive patronage of the national government." "We are not to attribute this prohibition of a national religious establishment [in the First Amendment] to an indifference to religion in general, and especially to Christianity, which none could hold in more reverence than the framers of the Constitution.... Probably, at the time of the adoption of the Constitution, and of the Amendments to it... the general, if not the universal, sentiment in America was, that Christianity ought to receive encouragement from the State."
Judge Joseph Story (1779-1845)
Supreme Court Justice (1812-1845)

⇨ Timeless Teaching Tips

"Christianity must be considered as the foundation upon which the whole structure rests. Laws will not have not permanence or power without the sanction of religious sentiment, without a firm belief that there is a Power above us that will reward our virtues and punish our vices. In this age there will be no substitute for Christianity: that, in its general principles, is the great conservative element on which we must rely for the purity and permanence of free institutions. That was the religion of the founders of the Republic, and they expected it to remain the religion of their descendants. There is a great and very prevalent error on this subject in the opinion that those who organized this Government did not legislate on religion."

House Judiciary Report in 1854

"The foundations of our society and our government rest so much on the teachings of the Bible that it would be difficult to support them if the faith in their teachings would cease to be practically universal in our country."

Calvin Coolidge (1872-1933)
30th President of the United States (1923-1929)

"Christianity, general Christianity, is and always has been a part of the common law... Thus this wise legislature framed this great body of laws, for a Christian country and Christian people... No society can tolerate a willful and despiteful attempt to subvert its religion, no more than it would to break down it laws - a general, malicious and deliberate attempt to overthrow Christianity, general Christianity."

Supreme Court of Pennsylvania
Updegraph vs The Commonwealth 1824

It's Been Said 👓

"The Congress ... desirous ... to have people of all ranks and degrees duly impressed with a solemn sense of God's superintending providence, and of their duty, devoutly to rely... on His aid and direction... Do earnestly recommend... a day of humiliation, fasting and prayer; that we may, with united hearts, confess and bewail our manifold sins and transgressions, and, by a sincere repentance and amendment of life ... and through the merits and mediation of Jesus Christ, obtain His pardon and forgiveness."

Continental Congress (1774-1781)
May 16, 1776

"When you become entitled to exercise the right of voting for public officers' let it be impressed upon your mind that God commands you to choose for rulers just men who will rule in the fear of God. The preservation of a republican government depends upon the faithful discharge of this duty; if the citizens neglect their duty and place unprincipled men in office, the government will soon be corrupted... If a republican government fails... it must be because the citizens neglect the divine commands, and elect bad men to make and administer the laws."

Noah Webster

 **Timeless Teaching Tips**

Science

"To suppose that the eye with all its inimitable contrivances... Could have been formed by natural selections, seems, I freely confess, absurd in the highest degree."
Charles Darwin (1809-1882)
British Naturalist – "Father of Evolution"

And those twelve stones, which they took out of Jordan, did Joshua pitch in Gilgal. And he spake unto the children of Israel, saying, When your children shall ask their fathers in time to come, saying, What mean these stones? Then ye shall let your children know, saying Israel came over this Jordan on dry land.
The Bible: Joshua 4:20-22
Joshua, Son of Nun (perhaps 1575 B. C. –1465 B. C.)
Led the Jews into the Promised Land

If a child can readily recognize a greater power and intelligence in a pattern of twelve stones, as Joshua assumed, then a child has more common sense than an evolutionist.
Tom Herzog (1937-   )
Beloved husband of the author

"I was a young man with unformed ideas. I threw out queries, suggestions, wondering all the time over everything; and to my astonishment the ideas took like wildfire. People made a religion of them."
Charles Darwin

It's Been Said 👓

"Why, then, should we who believe in Christ be so surprised at what God can do with a willing man in a laboratory? Some things must be baffling to the critic who has never been born again."
George Washington Carver (1864-1943)
African American Scientist
Discovered over 300 uses for peanuts

"How can anyone lose who chooses to become a Christian? If, when he dies, there turns out to be no God and his faith was in vain, he has lost nothing – in fact, he has been happier in life than his nonbelieving friends. If, however, there is a God and a heaven and hell, then he has gained heaven and his skeptical friends will have lost everything in hell!"
Blaise Pascal (paraphrased) 1623-1662
Father of the Science of Hydrostatics"

"The more I study nature, the more I stand amazed at the work of the Creator."
Louis Pasteur (1822-1895)
Great Scientist
Discovered diseases are spread by bacteria

"The undevout astronomer must be mad!"
William Herschel (1738-1822
Outstanding Astronomer,
Recognized Double Stars and Discovered Uranus.

"All human discoveries seem to be made only for the purpose of confirming more and more strongly the truths come from on high and contained in sacred writings.
John Herschel (1792-1871), Son of William Herschel
Outstanding Astronomer, Discovered over 500 New Nebulae

 **Timeless Teaching Tips**

Worldview

"Nonviolence is the answer to the crucial political and moral questions of our time; the need for man to overcome oppression and violence without resorting to oppression and violence."
Martin Luther King, Jr. (1929-1968)
American Civil Rights Leader

"Whoever shall introduce into public affairs the principles of primitive Christianity will change the face of the world."
Benjamin Franklin

"History fails to record a single precedent in which nations subject to moral decay have not passed into political and economic decline. There has been either a spiritual awakening to overcome the moral lapse, or a progressive deterioration leading to ultimate national disaster."
Douglas MacArthur (1880-1964)
Great American General

"The thought of modern industry in the hands of Christian charity is a dream worth dreaming. The thought of industry in the hands of paganism is a nightmare beyond imagining."
President Theodore Roosevelt

"It is contrary to the spirit of Christianity and the civilization which Christianity has produced in the Western world."
United States Supreme Court, February 29, 1892
Church of the Holy Trinity v. United States

"no person...believing in Jesus Christ shall be troubled...for his or her religion."
Toleration Act 1636

It's Been Said 👓

God and the Bible

"All the good from the Saviour of the World is communicated through this Book; but for the Book we could not know right from wrong. All the things desirable to man are contained in it."
Abraham Lincoln

"The New Testament is the very best book that ever was or ever will be known in the world."
Charles Dickens

"In all my perplexities and distresses, the Bible has never failed to give me light and strength."
Robert E. Lee

"The Bible is the best Book in the world."
John Adams (1735-1806)
2nd President of the United States (1797-1801)

"The first and almost the only Book deserving of universal attention is the Bible. I speak as a man of the world to men of the world; and I say to you, Search the Scriptures!"
John Quincy Adams (1767-1848)
6th President of the United States (1825-1829)

"The Bible is for the Government of the People, by the People, and for the People."
John Wycliffe (1320-1384)
Leading English Philosopher

"Today happens to be the Lord's Day, so I will quote you something from my Bible: "See that ye love one another as I have loved you."
Ludwig van Beethoven (1770-1827)
One of the World's Greatest Composers

⇨ Timeless Teaching Tips

"I believe in the Holy Scriptures, and who so lives by them will be benefitted thereby."

General Ulysses S. Grant
Commander of the Union Army in the American Civil War (1860-1865), Later President of the United States (1869-1877

"It is impossible to mentally or socially enslave a Bible-reading people. The principles of the Bible are the groundwork of human freedom."

Horace Greeley (1811-1872)
American Newspaper Publisher

"Of the Divine character of the Bible, I think no man who deals honestly with his own mind and heart can entertain a reasonable doubt."

Simon Greenleaf

"What doth the Lord require of thee but to do justly and to love mercy, and to walk humbly with thy God?"

Warren Gamaliel Harding (1865-1923)
29th President of the United States (1921-1923)
quoting Micah 6:8 from the Bible

"That book (in reference to the Bible), Sir, is the Rock upon which our republic rests."

Andrew Jackson
7th President, founder of Democratic Party

Of the Bible: "a book worth more than all the other books that were ever printed."

Patrick Henry (1736-1799)
Statesman, Orator, Politician, Administrator

It's Been Said 👓

Important Quotes of Famous People

"But we have forgotten God. We have forgotten the gracious Hand which preserved us in peace, and multiplied and enriched and strengthened us; and we have vainly imagined, in the deceitfulness of our hearts, that all these blessings were produced by some superior wisdom and virtue of our own."
President Abraham Lincoln

"This means as the long night of paganism descends on Western nations, we as believers are afforded an even greater opportunity to share the faith that burns within us."
Dr. James C. Dobson
Christian Leader 1980's through present

"Lord, with glowing heart I'd praise Thee For the bliss Thy love bestows; For the pardoning grace that saves me, And the peace that from it flows. Help, O God, my weak endeavor"
Frances Scott Key (1779-1843)
Wrote the Star Spangled Banner

"I thank God for my handicaps, for, through them, I have found myself, my work, and my God."
Helen Keller (1880-1968)
Deaf-Blind Author/Lecturer

"Alexander, Caesar, Charlemagne, and myself founded empires; but upon what foundation did we rest the creations of our genius? Upon force! But Jesus Christ founded His upon love; and at this hour millions of men would die for Him."
Napoleon Bonaparte I (1769-1821)
Emperor of West and Central Europe early 1800's

⇨ Timeless Teaching Tips

"It was the Lord who put into my mind (I could feel His hand upon me) the fact that is would be possible to sail from here to the Indies."
Christopher Columbus (1451-1506)
Great Navigator, Discovered America 1492)

"It is expected they will come out over the Neck tonight, and a dreadful battle must ensue. Almighty God, cover the heads of our countrymen, and be a shield to our dear friends"
Abigail Adams
Wife of 2nd President, John Adams
Mother of 6th President, John Quincy Adams

"Child Jesus came to earth this day,
To save us sinners dying
And cradled in the straw and hay
The Holy One is lying. "
Hans Christian Andersen (1805-1875)
Denmark's most famous author

"Nor is this spiritual and moral disease to be healed by a better education, a few external, transient thoughts. It requires the hand of the great Physician, the Lord Jesus Christ. "
John Armstrong
Astronaut, Congressman: United States Senator

"I believe that Jesus, the Lord, became in the flesh a sacrificer and a sacrifice for sin; a satisfaction and price paid to the justice of God; a meriter of Glory and the Kingdom; a pattern of all righteousness; a preacher of the Word, which Himself was; "
Sir Francis Bacon (1561-1626)
English Philosopher and Statesman

"We think it is incumbent upon this people to humble themselves before God on account of their sins. "
John Hancock 1737-1793)
First Signer of America's Declaration of Independence

It's Been Said

"Our Saviour would love at no less rate than death; and from the supereminent height of glory, stooped and debased Himself to the sufferance of the extremest of indignities, and sunk himself to the bottom of abjectness, to exalt our condition to the contrary extreme."
Robert Boyle (1627-1691)
Irish Scientist, "Father of Modern Chemistry"

"We believe that the first time we're born, as children, it's human life given to us; and when we accept Jesus as our Savior, it's a new life. That's what "born again" means."
James Earl "Jimmy" Carter (1924-)
39th President of the United States (1977-1981)

"We have grasped the mystery of the atom and rejected the Sermon on the Mount."
Omar Bradley (1893-1981)
American General in World War II
Commanded 1 Million Soldiers

"Remember that God is our only sure trust. To Him, I commend you.... My son, neglect not the duty of secret prayer."
Mrs. Mary Washington
George Washington's Mother

"Be assured, Gentlemen, that I entertain a proper sense of your fervent supplications to God for my temporal and eternal happiness." "May the same wonder-working Deity, who long since delivering the Hebrews from their Egyptian Oppressors planted them in the promised land whose providential agency has lately been conspicuous in establishing these United States as an independent Nation still continue to water them with the dews of Heaven."
George Washington

"...but I expect to find the solution to those problems just in the proportion that I am faithful in the study of the Word of God."
President Woodrow Wilson

⇨ Timeless Teaching Tips

"I trust in God that, through the merits and atonement of His Son, we may both be prepared for the inevitable change."
James Buchanan (1791-1868)
15th President of the United States of America (1857-1861)

"Work as if you were to live 100 years; pray as if you were to die tomorrow"
Benjamin Franklin, Statesman, Author, Scientist

"I am only one, but I am one. I cannot do everything, but I can do something. What I can do, I should do and, with the help of God, I will do!"
Everett Hale 1822-1909)
American Author
Wrote "The Man Without a Country"

"All confidence must be withheld from the Means we use; and reposed only on that GOD who rules in the Armies of Heaven, and without whose Blessing the best human Counsels are but Foolishness and all created Power Vanity"
John Hancock
Signer of the Declaration of Independence

"It is a great comfort to trust God even if His providence is unfavorable. Prayer steadies one, when he is walking in slippery places even if things asked for are not given."
Benjamin Harrison (1833-1901)
23rd President of the United States ((1889-1893)

"I have been driven many times upon my knees by the overwhelming conviction that I had nowhere else to go. My own wisdom, and that of all about me, seemed insufficient for that day."
Abraham Lincoln
16th President of the United States

It's Been Said 👓

"O holy trust! O endless sense of rest! Like the beloved John To lay his head upon our Saviour's breast"
Henry Wadsworth Longfellow
Most Famous American Poet of the 1800's
Author of "The Midnight Ride of Paul Revere"

"Our faith teaches that there is no safer reliance than upon the God of our fathers..."
William McKinley (1843-1901)
25th President of the United States (1897-1901)

"I do rejoice to walk in the love of God my heavenly Father "
Thomas Jonathan "Stonewall" Jackson (1824-1863)
Famous Confederate General of the Civil War (1860-1863)

"Worshipping God and the Lamb in the temple: God, for his benefaction in creating all things, and the Lamb, for his benefaction in redeeming us with his blood."
Sir Isaac Newton (1642-1727)
English Scientist who Discovered Laws of Gravity

"My Friends: There is one great God and Power that hath made the world and all things therein, to whom you and I and all people owe their being and well-being"
William Penn (1644-1718)
Founder of Pennsylvania

"Now, God be praised, that to the believing souls
Gives light in darkness, comfort in despair!"
William Shakespeare (1564-1616)
Great English Playwright

"We, ...by the Providence of Almighty God, ...(undertake) propagating of the Christian Religion to such people, as yet live in darkness and miserable ignorance of the true knowledge and worship of God..."
1606 - Charter of Virginia

⇨ Timeless Teaching Tips

"Powhatan, please to know that I worship only one God and serve but one king."
Captain John Smith (1580?-1631)

"We have this day restored the Sovereign to whom alone men ought to be obedient. From the rising to the setting of the sun may His kingdom come."
Samuel Adams (1722-1803)
Patriot, Politician, Leading Speaker, Congressman

"Let my heart, gracious God, be so affected with Your glory and majesty that I may...discharge those weighty duties which thou requirest of me.... Again, I have called on thee for pardon and forgiveness of sins...for the sacrifice of Jesus Christ offered on the cross for me. Thou gavest Thy Son to die for me; and hast given me assurance of salvation."
George Washington (1732-1799)

Practical Helps

Limited Resources	103
A Dozen Teaching Tips	111
Teaching with Homeschool Notebook Journals	120
Thoughts on Reading	124
Teaching Reading Comprehension	130
Adult Reading Difficulties	135
Building Spelling Success	138
Math Helps	141
About Rewards	148
Including Young Children in the Homeschool	151

Practical Helps

Limited Resources

Many homeschooling families often have limited resources. Here are some inexpensive hints for enhancing your children's education.

If your children are K-3, there is some really good news for you! Everything you need to teach them can be taught without a curriculum! There is a small set of books for under $15 that would be helpful, but not necessary. It is the *3 R Series* by Ruth Beechick and is available from most homeschool supply companies.

Now, let's get on with some ideas. Start by thinking of what you need to teach. Perhaps your list will look something like this: reading, math, basic writing skills and some understanding of science and history.

First, you will need some paper, crayons, pencils, scissors and glue. Save

Gather Supplies.

103

⇨ Timeless Teaching Tips

empty boxes and containers, pretty papers, magazines, newspapers, ribbons, and wrappings. With those simple tools you can design all kinds of assignments and crafts.

Use What You Have.

Then look around your house. There are plenty of things to count: silverware, toothpicks, pencils, pieces of paper, toys, blocks. You can make up story problems about your children. " John had two forks and Suzy had three. How many altogether?" Or "John and Suzy and Will each had three cars. How many altogether?" Have them write the number sentence (2+3=5 or 3 x 3 = 9). If the child loves cars and you want to teach him colors and numbers, make a cardboard box garage with several doors. Have each door labeled with a number and a color. One day have the cars go in the doors by color. Another day have the right number of cars go in each door. Encourage his play to be an extension of what you are teaching him.

Use a ruler, a clock, and a set of measuring cups to teach measurement of lines, time, and volume. Do a unit on simple tools (wheel, lever, inclined plane, screw, pulley) and try to find examples of these around your house and garage. Try to move something heavy with and without a lever. Your back yard and neighborhood provide a wonderful opportunity to explore the wonder of God's creation. In the spring or summer, get some seeds and plant a garden. In the fall, plant winter crops and prepare an area for next spring's garden. In the winter, grow some things indoors and plan your garden for next year.

Practical Helps

> ### The Bible Can Be a Text!

The Bible can be your very first textbook. If you have several copies of the same version, that's even better. If you don't, cuddle on the couch and look over each other's shoulder. Read aloud together and follow along with your finger like your grandmother did. That way the youngest will be able to see where you are reading and keep track. Every day read together. Ask questions about what you read. Tell your children what it says to you. If it touches your soul in a profound way, share that. If you see an application in their lives, tell them about it.

If your youngest is still learning to count, call attention to the numbers of the verses running down the left of the columns. Ask her to read them out loud, or read them with her. Ask her to find and tell what number comes before nine or after thirty. Have her start at three and count three more and see where she lands. Then say, "Three and three are six." Write the problem on a 3" x 5" card for her to think about. On the back write the fact with the answer. Check it out in other chapters of the Bible and see if the answer is always the same. Challenge her to show you one where it does not work. Do a different fact each day and quiz her occasionally using the cards.

For spelling, choose words from the passage of the day for each of your children. Have them incorporate them into writing a story, making a dictionary, or playing a word game. If there is any action in the passage, have your children role model what the story tells about. Discuss why they did things that way, how you do them today, why there is a difference.

⇨ **Timeless Teaching Tips**

Make Something to Show You've Learned.

Make books, displays or models of things you study. For example, when you study about seeds, make a model of the parts of a seed, a display of several sprouting seeds, and a book showing the parts of a plant: root, stem, leaf, flower. Older children may make chapter books. For plants, have them make one chapter on the parts of a plant (root, stem, leaf, flower), one chapter on seeds including their parts and various methods of propagation, one on the parts of the flower (petal, stamen, sepals, pistil), one on uses of plants and one on tips for growing plants. These books may be several pages folded and stapled in the middle, a three-ring binder adding pages as necessary, or a purchased book or blank scrapbook. Pages may be filled with charts, writing, photographs, drawings, or even pop-up, fold-out and look-under sections. For those who are not yet writing or are reluctant writers, pictures may be cut and pasted and then labeled with a few words or short sentences. Old magazines and workbooks are excellent sources of inexpensive pictures for illustrating your books.

Go to the library.

Finally head to the library. Go often and check out as many books as they will let you. Check out books from the children's section - picture books, non-fiction, and fiction. Ask the librarian to help you find some books of learning games. If the library has computers for public use, once a week stay long enough to let the children work on the computers. Monitor what they see! If there is a story hour, check out the book being read before you decide whether to go or not. Search the shelves for some kitchen

Practical Helps

science books, nature craft, and how-to books on any subject. Check out the video section. You may need to preview these, but there are some excellent educational videos and they are free! Many mega churches have excellent libraries as well. They would have good wholesome books and videos.

Once in a while think of a topic and ask the librarian to locate (in the interlibrary loan system) books, records, tapes, videos and/or games on that topic. Inundate yourselves in this topic. Read about it. Talk about it. Do one or more projects related to it. Make up a play, sing a song, write a book, or make a miniature scene or newspaper. Then show someone (grandparents, spouse, elderly, neighbors) what you've done.

> **Look for Lessons in Simple Things.**

Buy some popcorn. Record the weight and price. Figure out and record the per ounce price. Count the kernels you plan to pop. Predict how many you think will pop. Count the un-popped kernels. Count the fully popped ones. Try to pop the half-popped ones. Make a graph. Do it twice a week until that corn is gone and then try a different brand. By spring you should be experts on which popcorn is the best buy. In the fall make popcorn balls and for Christmas make caramel corn. In the spring plant some of the seeds and see if they will grow. Try planting other seed/food like sweet potatoes, dried peas and beans, apple or orange seeds, carrot tops, melon or pepper seeds. Try growing and taste testing several kinds of sprouts. Do some experiments to find out whether the sprouts do best in the dark or sunlight, dry or wet, cold or warm environments. Record your findings.

107

➡ Timeless Teaching Tips

Read Aloud Every Day.

Read aloud to your children every day. Read all kinds of books: biographies, picture books, and non-fiction books (elementary level). Read chapter books a little at a time. Talk about what you read. Think of projects related to what you read. Take a field trip. Many museums are free. Some zoos are inexpensive. Take on a family project of raising and saving enough money for an occasional treat. Let everyone do their share. Have a garage sale, make and sell cookies, or sell some seedlings in the spring.

Every Child Writes Every Day.

Have each child write in a journal every day. (The youngest may copy another child's or even draw a picture for you to label with his help.) Start with the date and a weather report. List the books you read or they listen to. Tell what you did or plan to do. Include feelings, dreams, and Bible verses you've learned. This does not have to be a polished production. A few words one day, more another. A few minutes one day, more another. Draw a picture one day, write a story another. Variety is pleasant, freedom is necessary. What is important is that each child write every day.

Teach your learners to use a dictionary, a phone book, an atlas, and how to read a map. Show them encyclopedias and how to use them. Get an almanac and investigate what it has to teach. Use the books in your house, the junk mail that comes, and the freebie papers that are endlessly available for lessons about reading, punctuation, morals, social skills, memorizing, whatever!

Practical Helps

Make a photo journal.

Have each child begin his own photo journal. Take pictures when they do projects, when you go on field trips or vacations. Have the children mount the pictures and write a caption consisting of a few words, a sentence or a paragraph. Take a class, if you can, and learn to design the pages.

Write a Cook book.

Have each child begin to create his own cookbook. As you teach him to cook, have him copy his favorite recipes. As he learns about measurements, have him half and double the recipe. He may want to record both on the back of the original. Take a picture of him cooking or show him with the final result. Let him look at several cookbooks to see how they are organized and have him copy the format in designing his own cookbook. Slip the recipes into a top loading page protector and keep them in a 3 ring binder. He is practicing skills and developing something that will stay with him into adult life.

Learn to Serve.

Get involved in service projects. Once a week take a homemade gift (a card, a loaf of bread, a seedling, a hug) to a resident in a nursing home. Offer to care for the child of a single parent for a few hours. Rake the lawn or shovel the walk of an elderly neighbor. Put love into practice with the whole family involved. Become a volunteer at a hospital or animal shelter. Serving is a wonderful opportunity to mature and develop skills.

⇨ Timeless Teaching Tips

Use Garage Sale Finds.

Comb through garage sales and flea markets for used books, games, and learning tools. You'll be surprised how much you can find for little money! Take the children along. They may see things you don't notice - or have ideas about how to use things you don't see a purpose for. Take a limited amount of money and stick to it. Dicker. Have fun. Take along some sandwiches and water and have a picnic in some park as you look over your treasures.

Love. Share. Be a family.

Most of all, love your children. Involve them in what you do. Share with them the things you know about or love to do. Share with them the things they love to do. Be a family and provide opportunity for learning to happen. Answer those hundreds of questions children ask by taking time to talk to them. If you don't know the answer, look it up in a book or encyclopedia.

Don't try to do all of these ideas in a week, a month, or even a year. Remember today is the beginning of the rest of your life. Plan today for a pleasant learning experience. Tomorrow do the same. You will soon find that you have piled up many happy learning times and your children have healthy curiosities and the skills to appropriately discover what they need to know. It isn't enough to teach them information. It is even more important to teach them where to find information and how to evaluate and process what they learn. Have fun together and you will be amazed at how much you all learn!

Practical Helps

A Dozen Teaching Tips

Learning can be greatly enhanced through the use of manipulatives of various kinds. These do not have to be expensive or elaborate, but variety and novelty are intriguing to children. Here are some ideas for you.

1 **1" and 1/2" Graph Paper** can be used to simplify many writing chores. When your child is beginning to print capital letters, use the 1" graph paper. Each letter fits nicely into one box. This is wonderful for the children who can't seem to keep the letters on the line. It seems easier to understand to put one letter in each box.

1/2" graph paper simplifies printing of lower case letters. When the child is first learning, have him make just the letters that fit in one box (a, c, i, n, o, r, s, u, v, w and so on). Later, he can print one letter in each box. For the letters g, p, q and y, only the tails will extend out of the box. The tall letters will take two boxes, too. You've got it!

⇨ Timeless Teaching Tips

1/2" graph paper is also helpful when teaching math. It is wonderful for keeping columns of figures in line (one numeral in each box). This is great for learners who are beginning to rename (borrow and carry) in addition and subtraction and also for the later stages of multiplication and division. The same paper is also helpful when teaching perimeter and area. Cut out rectangles of various sizes using the squares as a guide. To determine area, the child counts the full squares making it easy for him to understand the term six "square feet" or three "square inches." For perimeter he must count only the outer edges of the squares which make up the border of the figure. To make this concept come alive, walk around a play area repeating, "We are walking the perimeter." When you have completed the circuit, point to the area you have circled and tell the children: "We have walked around that area. We walked the perimeter. Now you may play in that whole area." The difference between area and perimeter will be easy for them to understand. If they forget, just ask them if they would rather play on the perimeter or in the area. For added interest, see if he can find and state a formula for when the perimeter is the same as, larger than, and smaller than the area.

Children also enjoy coloring the paper - each square a different color - or in an interesting pattern. Ask him to find the smallest number of colors he can use and still never have the same color touch itself. An older student can color over the top of his already colored paper pressing very hard with black or paint over it with India ink. He may then scratch out a design in the top layer and the colors will show through with a very pleasant effect.

Practical Helps

If you have difficulty locating this multi-purpose paper, contact Miller Pads and Paper. 2840 Neff Rd. • Boscobel, WI 53805 • 608-375-2181. They are a homeschooling family and also have spill-proof paint and other wonderful papers and art supplies. For more ideas on how to use this paper, see the author's mini book, *Graph Paper as an Educational Tool.*

2 Print and Paste Spelling Some children have great difficulty writing and yet need to practice spelling. Here is a solution. On several days have him use 1/2" graph paper to practice his printing. Cut the squares apart. Have him sort them and keep only his best letters - the ones which are easy to read. Then he can paste these letters into words. To reuse the letters several times, cover the front with contact paper and the back with library glue or other temporary glue. If you use library glue, let the glue dry for a few minutes before cutting. Mount the letters on a sheet of wax paper or a smooth slick surface such as a whiteboard. (If you want lots of this wonderful whiteboard, see hint below.) Use the letters to practice spelling words without writing. If you are doing spelling with a child who is not yet printing legibly, have him stamp the letters in the squares with letter stamps or use letter stickers. Magnetic letters are great for spelling without writing, too.

3 Write and Wipes You can make your own nice and very inexpensive whiteboards for dry erase markers. Just purchase a 4' by 8' sheet of bathroom wallboard (about $12) and cut to appropriate sizes. 8 1/2" x 11" or 10" x 12" is great for individual use. One 4' x 8' piece will make forty 8 1/2" x 11" boards. The 8 1/2" x 11" size may be drilled with three holes and

⇨ **Timeless Teaching Tips**

kept handy in a notebook. Mount larger boards on the wall or even use them on the floor. Vis A Vis™ markers, china markers, and erasable crayons also work well on these surfaces. Children love using these for doing math, drawing pictures, practicing spelling and all other writing or drawing activities. Use Vis A Vis™ markers for drawing what you want to remain and then dry erase markers for less permanent materials. For instance, use Vis A Vis™ markers for drawing a road and dry erase markers for the cars; use Vis A Vis™ markers to print words and dry erase for dividing them into syllables; use Vis A Vis™ markers to print out a Bible reference and dry erase to put in the Bible verse; use Vis A Vis™ markers to draw half a picture and have the child finish the details with dry erase. You need to know, though, if you leave dry erase marker for a week or two, it will become permanent! Erase it today or tomorrow! It is also permanent on cloth.

4 Miniatures for Visual Memory, Math and Language
Children love tiny things! Make a collection of things that are naturally very small (screw, hairpin, paper clip, penny, etc.) and miniature things from your children's toys or a craft shop. Keep this collection in a clear plastic shoe box or divided craft box. Use these items to solicit speech by asking the child to name and describe them. Help him build his vocabulary by asking the child to pick up the item you name or describe. To increase verbalization, encourage the child to talk about the item, describe it or its functions, or make up a story using several of the items. To build visual memory, have the child choose three to five items. Name them or have him do so, then move them around and ask him to name them one more time. Then hide them, or have him close or cover his eyes. While he cannot see what you

Practical Helps

are doing, remove one or two items. Have him open his eyes and tell what you have removed. Gradually increase the number of items and the amount of time before he sees them. Have him count them, make up story problems about them, or have him use them as counters in figuring out math problems. As a final clincher, show him the items, hide them, then sing a song or recite a joke before you show them again and ask what is missing. When the child can do that you know his memory is good enough for most life tasks! For more help in this area, see author's product *School in a Box*.

5 Auditory Memory Building auditory memory can be as simple as having the child recite a series of numbers or letters. Children who have very poor auditory memory may need visual clues at first. Let them see and hear the series. Start with a series where the child can be successful, even if that means the child repeats only one number immediately after hearing it. Gradually increase the length of the series and the time delay before he repeats it and remove the visual clue. Never increase until the child is successful at least 80% of the time. This can become a game to fill little minutes waiting in the car or at a doctor's office. Recite one letter or number per second. Wait the same number of seconds before giving the child a signal to respond. In most instances, the child will recite the sequence. If he is to write the sequence, have him put his pencil on the floor until you give the signal. Older children and adults should be able to recite a sequence of seven. For variety, sentences can be used. A child who is at the stage of remembering a sequence of three letters or numbers should be able to recite a sentence of five to six words. The meaning of the sentence aids the memory. When my children got pretty good at this, I added a distracter. At first

⇨ Timeless Teaching Tips

I hummed and moved around the room for a few seconds while they held the figure in their mind. Eventually I sang and acted silly and made them wait 30 seconds. Like visual memory, this is an important life skill that is too seldom taught.

6 **Memorization Review Card Pack** Use 3" x 5" cards - or cut them in half. Print (or type and paste on) one verse or passage per card. Put the reference on the back. Punch a hole in each card in a uniform spot near an edge. Purchase a single notebook ring (available at discount or office supply stores). Put the cards on the ring and keep handy! Make a new ring for each year. Review them all occasionally. This technique can be used for letter recognition for young children, math facts practice, Bible verse memory, or any activity which normally uses flash cards. Just write the answer on the back. These flash-cards- on-a-ring won't get lost or damaged as easily as others!

7 **Page Protectors** Purchase inexpensive page protectors sold in packages of 50 or 100. Slip any workbook page or worksheet inside. If the page is too large to fit inside the page protector, cut off the side with notebook holes and slip the remainder over the workbook page - even if it is still in the book! Use dry erase markers, china markers, Vis A Vis™ pens, or erasable crayons to write on the plastic. One child can do the sheet over and over or use it for several children. Any workbook page becomes a reusable activity sheet! These page protectors are also wonderful for keeping track of children's art work and writing samples which are not on standard size paper.

Practical Helps

8 **Food Fractions** Fractions can be easily seen when using fruit that normally come in sections such as oranges and grapefruit. Section an orange. Count the sections. Let's say there are twelve. Give one to one child. It is easy for him to see that he has one of the twelve sections of an orange. Write 1/12 to show him what he has. Read it as "One of 12 or one-twelfth." Now give him four more. Write 4/12. Read it as "Four of twelve or four-twelfths." Ask him how many he has now. He will say 5. Remind him that these are five of the original twelve and ask him to write the fraction that tells how many he has. He should write 5/12. The next day cut an apple in half. Ask him how many pieces there are. Give him one of them. Tell him that he has one of the two halves. Write 1/2. Call it, "One of two or one-half." The next day do oranges again. (Will every orange have the same number of sections?) Another day cut a round pizza into equal segments. Still another day cut a pie into sixths or eighths. Each time ask a question and write the number sentence to show the problem and the correct answer such as: "You have one of three or one-third. I give you one more. Now you have two of three or two-thirds. The number sentence looks like this: 1/3 + 1/3 = 2/3." "You have five of twelve or five-twelfths. I take away three of them or three-twelfths. Now you have two-twelfths left. The number sentence looks like this: 5/12 - 3/12 = 2/12." (Do not worry about equivalent fractions at this time.) Gradually increase the number of problems you have him do and have him write the number sentence. Go through a similar procedure every day for two weeks and your child will have a much better understanding of fractions.

⇨ Timeless Teaching Tips

9 **Rub-on Art** You will need: large sheets of a fairly thin paper such as newsprint or typing paper and broken crayons with the paper removed. Look around the house for textures like a screen, a wall socket, brand names or logos on appliances, bumps on a floor runner, etc. Or gather leaves or cut shapes from thin cardboard. Cover the texture with paper. Hold the crayon horizontally on the paper and rub across the texture. You will transfer its design onto your paper. You may also trace over the letters or words you make with cornmeal (see following).

10 **Colored Cornmeal** You can color cornmeal by adding food coloring. Put some cornmeal in a bowl and add food color. Stir together until the color is uniform and pleasing. Spread it out and let it dry. (In damp climates, spread on cookie sheets and store in a 150 oven for two hours.) This can be used in any activity that calls for colored sand. Or use some of these ideas:
- Put colors in layers in a nicely shaped jar with a lid.
- Draw a picture or design. Paint the area which could be one color with glue. Sprinkle on the cornmeal and then cover a different area for a different color and repeat.
- Write words or draw shapes with a thin line of glue. Use large designs and/or print with large letters so the glue does not run together and splotch. Sprinkle on cornmeal and allow to dry without touching. These can then be used in the rub-on designs described above. Words printed this way are also good for tracing for kinesthetic (hands on) learners.
- Fill the bottom of a cake pan with this cornmeal and draw designs or print letters or words for kinesthetic practice.

11 **Flash Card Games** Cut 3" x 5" cards in half and make flash cards for letter or number recognition, reading or math. These may be color coded by coloring the **end** of the cards with

Practical Helps

a permanent marker. These store perfectly in a two-pound cheese box (like Velveeta™). You can keep enough cards for a whole classroom in one or two boxes. Children of different ages and abilities can play many games together. Use any blank game board for all to play together, but let each work with a pack of flash cards appropriate for his age, learning ability and the subject you want him to practice in. Thus one child can be memorizing math facts while another polishes science vocabulary and a third practices reading short vowel words, yet all are playing the same game at the same time. To earn a roll of dice and a turn, the child must give the correct answer to one (or more) flash cards.

12 **Dot to Dot Books** Young children delight in dot-to-dot books, but you can extend their use in many ways. First of all, be aware that there are now available many very easy dot-to-dot books starting with 1-5 and 1-10. There are also ABC dot-to-dots for the children who are learning letter names and sequence. When your children get bored with the level they are working on, but still need more practice, have them work the dot-to-dot backwards! To do this, they first have to locate the biggest number. That is difficult enough for some children, but it forces them to grasp the "big picture" before they begin to work. Also try having them create their own dot-to-dots for friends or siblings. Make it fairly simple shapes. Maybe they could count by twos or fives or tens. Be creative! Let them think of new ways to apply old skills.

When learning is fun, children love to learn and teachers love to teach!

Timeless Teaching Tips

Teaching with Homeschool Notebook Journals Progress for All to See

Teaching with notebooks is an easy, inexpensive way to organize your children's activities. It combines planning, teaching, and record-keeping into one simple system. All you need is a 3-ring binder with dividers for each person (age 2 or 3 to 99), blank paper with and without lines, pens, pencils, markers, magazines, scissors, glue sticks, time, and imagination! These can be effective at home, school, or church.

Each person keeps a notebook of his work. For younger children, it can contain pages they work on every day. For elementary age and above, it may contain one page per subject per week. For all ages it holds lists of books read, maps, mini-posters, photographs of projects and field trips, drawings, charts and graphs, and whatever else you or the student decides needs to be kept for reference or nostalgia.

Practical Helps

Notebook Headings:

BE SURE TO DATE EVERY PAPER!

Section Titles Everyone Uses:
Scripture: Record scriptures for memorization, meditation.
Prayer: (needs and answers) Record and date prayer requests and their answer
Books Read: (or read to them)
Projects: keep photographs of all projects they participate on.

Section Titles for Preschoolers
ABC's - a page or two per letter, labeled; collect other letters or pictures of objects that begin with that sound.
Colors - a page or two per color, labeled; collect pictures of objects that color, trace color words.
Numbers - a page or two per numeral, labeled with correct number of objects in a box and number word. Collect pictures of sets of objects.
Shapes - a page or two per shape; collect pictures which emphasize that shape.
Projects - pages for photographs of projects the child participates in; label with a paragraph description of what he did
Bible or Memory Work - copy of Bible verses memorized, illustrated by the child to assist memory.

Section Titles for Primary Grades
My Own Dictionary - include words the child learns to spell, or adds to his spoken vocabulary; allow the child to illustrate it to assist his memory.
My Stories - copies of stories the child writes.
About Me - journal or stories about things the child likes.

➡ Timeless Teaching Tips

My Book of Numbers - a page a week to show what he is learning about numbers and math.
Books We Read - list of the books which are read to him.
Books I Read - list of the books he reads.
My Prayers - Prayers he writes, list of his special prayers.
Projects - photographs of projects he completes; he writes or dictates descriptive sentence or paragraph.

Section Titles For
Intermediate Grades and Teens

Dictionary - include words he learns to spell or adds to his spoken vocabulary
Creative Writing - copies of his writing
Letters - copies of letters to editor, senator, etc.
Math - a paper a week to show progress
Reading List - a list of books he reads
History - a paper a week, or a brief report of each topic studied; photos as appropriate
Science - a paper a week, or a brief report of each topic studied; photos as appropriate.
Projects - photographs of projects he attempts or completes.
Prayers And Their Answers - record and date request and answer.
Soft Thoughts
Questions I'd Like to Ask
Bible Passages that Speak to Me
Me: Who I Am
Me: Who I Want to Be

Practical Helps

**Other Topic Ideas
Pithy Truths From the Word of God
Who I Am, What I Think, What I'm Good At...
Prayer List with answers. Be sure to include dates!
Soft and Gentle Thoughts
Things I'm Not too Sure Of
Things I'd Like to Do Someday
My Heroes: People I Respect and What I Like About Them
Bible Studies
Personality Characteristics I Think are Admirable
Sketches I've Made, Pictures I like
Attributes of God - Who He is; What He is Like
Sermon Notes
Favorite Scriptures
Little Lessons From My Life**

This is an exciting way to simplify and organize. Occasionally invite grandparents and other loved ones over and spend an evening reminiscing over the books. If they live far away, mail the book and ask for comments. Save the books; pass them on as your children marry. The newlyweds can get better acquainted and laugh over the past and think about the possibilities for their own children!

Nobody said raising children was easy, but it shouldn't be drudgery either. The most important thing is to love your children, prepare them to discover and carry out God's call on their lives, and teach them what they need to know to succeed as adults. This system makes it easier! For more on this, see the author's mini book *SIMPLIFIED Homeschool and RecordKeeping* and *Luke's Life and Luke's School Lists.*

 Timeless Teaching Tips

Thoughts on Reading

What? Me? Teach Reading?

| **Panic sets in.** | Many parents are afraid of teaching their own children to read. They see struggling readers |

and think, "If that is the result of a professional effort, maybe this job is too much for me." Or perhaps their child has reached a certain age, covered a phonics program, or come out of a public school and still is not reading and the parent begins to panic. Tension starts when someone asks, "Isn't Johnny reading yet?" or when the child is called on to read out loud and cannot. It begins in the pit of the stomach and spills over into classes and conversations. The problem is that panic is a negative emotion with no redeeming virtues. It affects everyone it touches and can, indeed, create problems where none existed before.

Many parents, under pressure from friends, family, "experts," and self-criticism, increase pressure, spend more time in reading instruction, try several phonics programs, threaten and cajole. The learner reacts by concentrating on his inadequacy and develops an "I can't" attitude. As tensions increase learning

Practical Helps

ceases. The child is forced through a learn-to-read program and becomes a struggling reader who never chooses to read because it has been such an ordeal to read and he associates reading with great unpleasantness. Now what?

One mom who was considering my own reading program began to explain her failures with teaching her child to read. They had already been through three reading programs without success. I asked how old the child was. Six! They couldn't have given any of the reading programs more than four months unless they started when this boy was four or younger. Now they were ready to add one more frustrating experience in the learn-to-read game.

My prescription for this tense home was to drop all reading instruction and learn to read programs for at least six months while providing loving and happy experiences reading aloud wonderful books. When he was ready to try again, she would do well to choose a fun and unique approach to learning-to-read such as the author's *The Scaredy Cat Reading System*. There is plenty of time for young learners to acquire the skill of reading. We never ask adults *when* they learned to read!

Take a Break!

There is no magic rule that says children should read by age six. Historically it was never so. When our schools were founded, it was expected that every child would learn to read - by age twelve! Today we consider our children to be delayed learners if they are not reading fluently by age six or seven. As if to prove

Every Child Should Be Able to Read By Age Twelve!

⇨ Timeless Teaching Tips

us right we can readily point to neighbors, classmates or relatives who are reading at an early age. The truth is that some children can and do learn to read very young. Others are not ready for reading until they are eight, nine, ten or even eleven.

One man who did not learn the alphabet until he was nine years old and did not learn to read until he was eleven became President of the United States of America. His name? Woodrow Wilson! We used to call them "late bloomers." Now we label them "learning disabled." Late bloomers only meant they started late; now we expect them to have problems all their lives. It is not necessarily so.

God Wrote a Book.

I believe everybody can and will learn to read if given the opportunity, instruction, time and encouragement. God wrote a book. He desires for every person to learn to read and have access to that book. But God has an enemy who wishes for us to fail and unfortunately, at times, the very people who desire for their children to read make it impossible for them to learn.

Let's look at some ways to help increase the likelihood that your children will become good readers:

First of all, read to them. I often say, "Read to your children until they are reading aloud to their children." Read picture books, chapter books, and **Read to Your Children.**

non-fiction books. Read stories, riddles, jokes, and poems. Read good literature, the Sunday funnies, the Bible, and road signs. Read biographies, novels, mysteries, and humor. Let your child

Practical Helps

see you reading for information and for pleasure. Your child will be more interested in reading if he sees that reading is important to the adults in his life. It will make an even greater impact on him if he sees that adults enjoy reading.

Try to make reading instruction time a pleasant experience. Choose your reading program carefully.

Make Reading Fun.

Many programs that claim to be phonetic are not and many that claim to be multi-sensory are dull and uninviting. Most phonics programs don't appeal to the child's need for fun and logic. Others lack organization and systematic flow. Few give the child enough time to assimilate information or let you know when to add new concepts. Whole language programs that surround the child with the written word may leave him unable to attack long unfamiliar words.

Teach Reading Comprehension Early!

Don't leave the teaching of comprehending what you read until the child has reached the third grade level in reading. Reading comprehension is best taught as the child learns to read and spell words. The little words are full of multiple and rich meanings. Take the word *can*. I *can* do something. I put the garbage in a *can*. I *can* tomatoes and green beans. A friend at the office lost his job and we say, "He was *can*ned." The children are becoming boisterous and we say, "*Can* it!" *Can* you think of others? Try **run, sand, hand, tap, play, time, fine,** and **win**. When you work on vowels that say their names in words (long vowels), work on homonyms (words which sound the same, but are spelled differently and have different meanings) such as pain/pane, mane/main, road/rode,

⇨ Timeless Teaching Tips

and brake/break. Real reading is far more than decoding and pronouncing groups of letters. It is getting ideas from the printed page. (See next section for more about this!)

Approach Reading from Many Angles.
When you read aloud, don't demand that he sit still and listen, but let him color, play with construction toys or building blocks, or finger paint while you read aloud. Bring home some books on science experiments, nature projects, or other active project-oriented books. When you are reading for your own pleasure, get excited about what you are reading and say," Listen to this!" Then proceed to read a funny or interesting passage. Take trips to the library and check out books. Spend time browsing in used book stores. Subscribe to some good children's magazines. Begin to read a book out loud, stop at a very crucial point and leave the book lying around. Get Dad involved in reading aloud. Play word games.

Read Aloud Together.
Choral reading is a lost art. Get several copies of a book, or a passage from the Bible. Every night at the supper table, read out loud in unison. Read just a little faster than is comfortable for the struggling reader. Run your finger under the line of print for the younger learners. Read one passage until the family is almost reciting it aloud, Then change the passage and build the speed a little. Many children learn to read best by this type of repetition.

The book *Amusing Ourselves to Death*: says this about the correlation between television, reading, and thinking:

Practical Helps

Postman's thesis is that different types of media encourage different ways of thinking. The printed word requires sustained attention, logical analysis, and an active imagination. But television, with its fast-moving images, encourages a short attention span, disjointed thinking, and purely emotional responses.

An article in the July 1995 issue of *Reader's Digest* has this to say about reading aloud to children:

"Numerous studies, including recent reports by The Center for the Study of Reading and the National Council of Teachers of English, confirm that reading to children builds vocabulary, stimulates imagination, stretches the attention span, nourishes emotional development, and introduces the textures and nuances of the English language. Reading aloud is, in essence, an advertisement for learning to read."

In summary, if your child isn't reading yet, don't panic! That can only delay the process. Determine whether he needs a break from the pressure of "reading instruction." Increase his pleasant experiences with books and reading. Limit time spent in front of a screen (television, mindless computer games, etc.). Carefully select a phonics program that is systematic, logical, fun, and involves the child's senses, personality, humor and movement. Enjoy books with your child!

⇨ **Timeless Teaching Tips**

Teaching Reading Comprehension

Reading comprehension refers to reading for meaning and making judgements rather than merely word calling.

> **Teach Comprehension Early.**

It is important that you don't wait until the child is reading chapter books before you begin to teach comprehension. Learning to get meaning from writing will be much harder if it has not been learned as a natural part of reading. Some people are satisfied when beginning readers say the right sounds or name the correct word. They need to check to see if the child is getting meaning from the printed page. When you are teaching beginning reading skills, make sure the child is understanding that translating symbols into sounds (reading) has the purpose of getting meaning and understanding concepts, not just word calling. In my *Scaredy Cat Reading System,* I start with teaching short ("scared") vowel words. We begin with the vowel A. We will list words like pat, can, ram, and bag. I encourage the child to think of many meanings for these tiny words. A pat can be a small piece of butter, what you do to the pie crust, or what you do to burp a baby. ***Can*** might be a verb: "I *can* go" or "Mom will *can* the tomatoes." ***Can***

Practical Helps

may refer to what the boss does to an inefficient employee. Or it can be a noun: Put the peanuts in the *can.* ***Bag*** may be something you carry the potatoes in or what a hunter does to game - which brings up the many meanings of *game!* Are you game for this?

Here are some ideas to help you use every opportunity to stretch your child's understanding of simple words and put them into a context. Add meaning to a word by having your child give a sentence using the word, or use it in a sentence yourself. Play with the words, be silly and have fun with words and with your child. Put several words in front of the child and have him find the one that rhymes with _____, or the one that could be used for _____. In these ways you are teaching that comprehension is a natural part of reading. Reading is not just turning a symbol into a sound; it is obtaining meaning from the printed page.

Stretch the Meanings.

As the child begins to work with sentences, continue the work with meaning. Ask the child to read the sentence to find out _____ (like what the cat is doing or where the hat is, or why the boy ran, etc.). Put several unrelated sentences in front of him and ask him to find the one that tells _____ (who ate the apple, where the hat was found, etc.) Cut out and separate three to five sentences that are sequential: Sam woke up. He dressed. He ate breakfast with the family. Then he went outside to play. Have the child put them in the correct sequence. When you are having fun throughout the day, occasionally stop and write down a sentence that tells what you are doing. Make it into a poster so show Dad or a letter to send to Grandma.

⇨ Timeless Teaching Tips

Think of other activities that will help the child understand that sentences are not just groups of words, but they are groups of words that express a thought.

Help Them Read for Fun and Information.

When the child is reading any passage for enjoyment or information, supply words he has trouble with and correct errors quickly, without fanfare or intermediate instruction. Save decoding ("sounding out"), instruction, and struggle for reading instruction time. When the goal is to get meaning from the printed page, make it as smooth and easy as possible even if you have to tell some of the words. You may need to have two "reading classes" or a reading time and a "phonics" time. During the phonics time, teach the child word attack skills and let him struggle a bit to sound out words. During the reading time, when he doesn't know a word, tell him what it is and keep him reading. Stopping to sound out words hampers comprehension, so decide in each instance whether the goal is learning to decode words or understanding the passage.

Five Finger Rule.

When your child is choosing a book to read, have him use the five finger test. When he reads a page, if he comes to a word he cannot read, have him put up a finger. If he uses all five fingers before he finishes the page, the book is too hard for him to read alone. It may be a "read to him" book, or you may need to be willing to give him a great deal of help as he reads it, but it is too hard for him to read without help.

Practical Helps

Realize that reading aloud with expression and reading silently are two very different skills. Most average and above children will be able to develop equal skill in both areas, but children who struggle with reading may be able to perfect only one of the two. Some may need to read aloud to get meaning,. Others may never be able to read aloud, but may read adequately silently even if they do not correctly decode every word. When you are reading aloud to a beginning reader and you come to a word he should recognize, point to it and encourage him to read it quickly. Then continue reading without repeating the word he has read. When your child is reading and comes to a word he does not know, he may then point to it and allow you to supply the missing word quickly and smoothly. Do not delay, but let him go on. This will keep the continuity and not lose the meaning of the passage. When you move into reading paragraphs and stories, here are more comprehension techniques that will help:

Two Kinds of Reading.

Always give a purpose for reading. "Read the story to find two problems the boy had in school." "Read the paragraph to find out what mother said." "Read to find out why _____."

Give a Reason to Read

Ask questions related to the basic parts of comprehension:

Ask Questions

What is the setting of the story?
Who are the main characters?

⇨ Timeless Teaching Tips

What is the plot?
  (What is happening? What problems are solved?)
What is the mood?
What is the purpose (moral) of the piece?
  Why did the author write it?
What is your response to the piece?
Is there a scripture that confirms the lesson of the piece?
How would a biblical character perceive the piece?
  (God, Moses, David, etc.)
Does the piece speak the truth?
Is the lesson taught or implied by the piece immoral or unscriptural?
What hidden assumptions are portrayed?
Evaluate the morality (world view, perspective) of the piece.

Reading must be more than word calling or it is meaningless. Reading can open doors to the past, to the minds of every great thinker who ever lived, to fantasy and imagination, to depths of feeling which are difficult to express. Reading can open doors, but word calling without meaning is a frustrating experience. Make a difference in your child's life. Teach him to understand what he reads!

Practical Helps

Adult Reading Difficulties

Some adults are still struggling readers. Though they have some ability, they find reading difficult and therefore avoid it whenever possible. This, in turn, causes them to make no progress and to perpetuate the problem. Here are some ideas to turn that around.

1. Try reading out loud. Some of us are auditory learners and when we **hear** the material, the concepts come easier.

2. Read phrase by phrase. Stop when you see a comma or period. Think about the groups of words. Make sure you understand the concepts conveyed in each phrase.

3. Stop at the end of each paragraph and try to summarize the thought. Write your summary in one or two sentences (on the side of the same page if you can). If one paragraph is too long for you to sustain the understanding, start by summarizing sentence by sentence, at least in your mind.

⇨ Timeless Teaching Tips

4. As you open the pages of scripture in particular, pray that God would reveal to you His meaning. He says if we need wisdom to ask for it. He is a "Man" of His Word!

5. Start building comprehension skills with easy-to-read material. Subscribe to a magazine designed for children or young people. *God's World* has weekly papers at several reading levels. Do the above activities with its articles. Read them to your children or grandchildren if you have any. Summarize each paragraph. When you get to where you can read a whole article with understanding, increase the reading difficulty. The next step would be the *Reader's Digest* and *Guideposts*. Both are full of short, simply written articles at an adult interest level.

As you read, look for key words and phrases that indicate sequence, importance or cause and effect. These include words like: first, next, then, foremost, most important, because, therefore, since, until, in summary, and in other words. These words often signal something worth remembering and understanding. See if you can answer the basic questions of who, what, when, and where. Then try to answer how and why. Look at bold headings. They often summarize what is to follow. Look for facts that support the main idea. Use the dictionary frequently to be sure you understand the meaning of the words used. Try to identify the mood of the author and his reasons for writing the material. If what you are reading has comprehension questions at the end, read them first and highlight the answers as you find them. Practice working from written instructions.

Practical Helps

Some adults who still struggle with reading skills have a **visual processing problem**. I required vision therapy **after** I had graduated from college and was teaching school. I had no depth perception and was on high risk car insurance. I got through college by reading for 15 minutes and sleeping for 10 to rest my eyes. Fortunately, I was a speed reader, but I could not sustain my focus and my eyes crossed after they tired of looking at the fine print. A few months of work at home and in the doctor's office left my problem permanently solved. Check out the College of Optometrists in Vision Development (www.covd.org or call 1-888-COVD-770) to find the name of someone in your area who specializes in vision therapy.

Reading is a skill. Like any other skill, it must be built step by step over a long period of time. To get better at reading, spend time daily reading from something you can enjoy and understand.

 **Timeless Teaching Tips**

Building Spelling Success

Many teens and adults continue to struggle with spelling. Here are some answers for those who are willing to work for success.

1. Work hard to memorize the high frequency words. (For source, see *Spelling Book* by Dr. Ed Fry below.) Say and spell and write **one word** until you can write it from memory. In this way, learn three words each day. Use color, magnetic letters or stamps to make it more fun. Spend one day a week and one week a month reviewing them. Learn them for life!

2. Choose three really tough words you are likely to use often (related to your interests, your spiritual life, etc.) and do the same thing with them. Spell each word as you normally would; then compare your spelling with the real and correct spelling. Make a mental note as to what you had to change. Once you have a word "mastered" enter it into your Spelling Notebook (see next hint).

3. To make a Lifetime Spelling Notebook, get a 3-ring binder with alphabetic dividers. Have a few pages behind each

Practical Helps

letter's divider. Enter the words you work on (after you are successful with them) onto the appropriate page in the book. Draw a little symbol or picture next to the word - perhaps one that signals what you had to correct to make the word right. Use color, designs and fancy writing to make the book special to you. Once a week, look at these words and refresh your memory on what you have learned. Once a month, write or type at least fifty of them.

4. Look up **every** word you are uncertain of. Add it to your Lifetime Spelling Notebook. For a while you may feel that you have to look up every word there is, but gradually your skill and confidence will increase.

5. Develop keyboard skills and use a word processor. Take all your important writing through a "spell-check." Make a list of the words it catches and choose your daily words from that list. That way you will know that you are studying words that are relevant.

Here are some excellent resources:

• There are several spelling principles worth learning. The author's *Scaredy Cat Reading System* contains many of them. Beyond that level, *Spelling Power* is the most comprehensive program I've seen. It contains 1st grade through high school under one cover. It is available through most home school suppliers.

• Use an electronic or phonetic dictionary as you write. An electronic dictionary makes it simple to look up a word and puts it at the touch of a button. They are available from local stores.

⇨ Timeless Teaching Tips

Franklin Learning Resources • 1-800-BOOKMAN carries these plus a whole electronic library.

• There is a phonetic key to the dictionary called *Word Finder*. It was originated and compiled by Marvin L. Morrison and published by Pilot Light, Stone Mountain, GA. ISBN 09608376-1-2. With this book (like the electronic dictionary) you can look up a word by how it sounds and find the real spelling. It should be available at your local book store. They may need to order it.

• Dr. Ed Fry's *Spelling Book* covers complete weekly lessons for grades 1 through 6 along with high frequency words, variant word forms and other information. You can also purchase his High Frequency Word List separately. He can be reached at: Laguna Beach Educational Books • 245 Grandview • Laguna Beach, CA 92651

Now, after all that, let me say one more thing; God can use even an adult who cannot spell for His glory in His Kingdom. Don't spend all your time working on your weaknesses to the neglect of your strengths. It is fine to work at improving your spelling - and math - and whatever - but it is far more important to be open to God's leading and ready to follow His call on your life. Maybe your poor spelling will be the very thing that attracts a spouse who loves to edit or makes someone else feel close enough to you to listen as you present them with the gospel!

Practical Helps

Math Helps

Sequence of Skills

Count by rote means just naming the numerals in the right sequence. You first teach our child to count by rote and then to count that number of objects, using one number for one object. When you begin to count objects, use real objects. When they can do this, switch to pictures of objects.

Conquer these skills in small bites.
        1, 2 (First count by rote. Then count two objects.)
        1 - 5 (count by rote, count 5 objects)
        1- 10 (count by rote, count 10 objects)
        1 – 20 (count by rote, count 20 objects)

Master the 1 on 1 relationship, that is, teach the child that each new number spoken stands for one more object. It is helpful to have him touch and move each object as he names the number - one number, one number word, move each new object to a new place so you can keep track of which ones you have counted.

⇨ Timeless Teaching Tips

Count by 2's, 5's, 10's, 11
This is easily taught with a Hundred Board. Use 1" graph paper cut into a 10 x 10 square. Print one numeral in each square. When you are doing the 2's, first lightly color every other number. It will be easy for you to see that the colored numbers make vertical rows, but let the child discover this for himself. Then have him name the colored numbers or the non-colored ones. He should start by counting by the even numbers: 2, 4, 6, 8, 10. It may be some time before he is ready to count the odd numbers.

Do the same thing when you are ready to work on the 5's 10's and 11's. Make a hundred board. Color in the squares of the multiples of the number you are working with. Notice the changing patterns. Marvel at the order that God has built into the system of numbers.

With older learners, make one number board to record the multiples of the numbers from 1 to 10. Choose a different color or method of marking the multiples of each number. For instance, circle in red the multiples of 2; trace in green the boxes of the multiples of 3, color yellow the multiples of 4, draw a blue triangle over the multiples of 5, and so on. In this way, you can begin to see which larger numbers are multiples of more than one small number. For example, 12 is a multiple of 2, 3, 4, and 6. This is a painless way of laying a foundation for understanding least common denominator when you are dealing with fractions.

Teach conservation of numbers. This concept means that moving the objects around without adding or removing any does not change the number of objects. For instance if you rearrange five objects, there are still five objects. The child must learn that

Practical Helps

the only way to change the number of objects is to put more or take some away (add or subtract). Until a child internalizes this concept, they cannot add or subtract with meaning.

Recognition of number patterns can be as simple as rolling a die and instantly recognizing the number it stands for without counting. If a child can do this **before** he learns to add and subtract, it will make his understanding of addition and subtraction jump miles ahead. Obtain 10-sided dice to carry this skill on past 6. (We sell them at joyceherzog.com.)

Addition
When you begin to teach addition, build on the counting skills and number recognition skills you have already developed.

Use real objects. Count the objects. Add one object. Count on from the original number. Do this until adding one is almost automatic. Then show how to write 2 + 1 = . Write all the problems from 0+1 to 9+1. Show both vertical and horizontal format. Do this kind of problem for a few minutes every day using objects to find the answer only when necessary.

Next teach adding 2 to a starting number. Do it in the same way you added one. Continue until the child can automatically add 2. Gradually go on to 3, 4, and so on. Don't rush through these! If the child masters each one before going on, you will have a solid foundation for the remainder of his math instruction!

Use pictures of objects. Count the objects in the picture. This is a transition step between counting objects and adding without anything to count.

➪ Timeless Teaching Tips

Teach "counting on" from original number:
    Count one set of objects.
    Name the number.
    Move to the next set of objects.
    Name the **next** number and keep counting.

Make or buy triangle flash cards. Cut triangles (about 5" on a side). On each, print one addition math fact in this way: Print the largest number (the sum) in the top corner. Print the two numbers that equal that sum - one in each of the side corners. Cover the number at the top and ask the child to name the total of the two numbers he sees. Uncover the numeral and have him check his answer. From this one card, you can do four math problems: If the total is 12, the other numbers may be 3 and 9. From this set of numbers, you can see that 3+9=12, 9+3=12, 12-3=9 and 12-9=3. This is a simple way to reinforce the commutative property of addition (the fact that, no matter which number you say first, 3 or 9 in this case, the total is the same). Practice the math facts until the child knows them quickly and easily before going on to new concepts. Start with the problems whose answer is 10 or less. Then master the problems whose answer is 18 or less (up to 9+9).

Subtract
To teach subtraction, use food: raisins, candy or cereal. Have the child count the number he has at first. Have him write that down. Have him remove some and count that number. Count how many are left. Have him write it this way: 6-4=2. If he does it correctly, he may eat the ones he "took away." Many children "hate" subtraction, but they won't if they learn it this way!

Practical Helps

Then show them the triangle flash cards and the relationship to the addition facts they've already mastered. They already KNOW the answers if they think about it right!

Multiply

Before you attempt teaching multiplication, do some addition of like numbers. For instance showing 3 children who each have 2 cars and ask how many they have all together. Do this several days in a row with real life people and objects. Talk about it as "Three two's are six" and "two 3 times is six."

Next, have the child write some of these problems out (2+2+2=6). When they are comfortable doing this, do one with 6 or 8 people and show how cumbersome it is to write 2 six times. Tell them there is a faster, easier way to think about this. Do one multiple addition with them, then show them how to write it as a multiplication problem. Start simple with ones they can "see" immediately. Do the multiple addition, say the fact, write the multiplication fact. (2+2+2=6 is the same as "two three times" or 3x2=6) Do a few every day until they are easy.

From this point, teach the understanding that doing anything "one time" doesn't change it. That is, one times anything is the same number you started with. Show them that if they are the only one who has 3, there are 3. Then write the "One Times Table:" 1x1=1, 1x2=2, 1x3=3, and so on to 1x9=9. At this time, it is fun to stretch their thinking a bit: ask them how many is 1 times one hundred. If they don't know right away, tell them one hundred. Do the same thing several times, giving interesting numbers like 150, one thousand, fifteen hundred, 777, and so on, until you are fairly sure they have the concept.

145

⇨ Timeless Teaching Tips

Next teach them that zero times anything is zero. This can be confusing. Ask if they have any cookies (when they don't!). Ask if you have given them any cookies (when you haven't). Ask them how many times you have given them cookies (zero). Ask how many cookies they have now (zero). Write the fact that 0x0=0. Not try it with another number. Ask them if they have 7 cookies. When they say no, tell them that they have 7 cookies zero times, and ask them, "How many cookies in all?" Do this in small doses daily until they understand or you give up! It will come eventually, but may have to wait!

At this point it is fun to begin to ask questions like: how many legs on 4 chickens, wheels on two motorcycles, eyes on 5 cats, etc. You may do this just to spur the thinking, or also have the child write the problem and the answer.

Doing the 2's is easy if they know the doubles in addition or can count by two. Knowing 6x2 is simply counting by two six times. Doing the 5's times table comes next because the children have already learned to count by 5's. Then the tens and 11's. At that point it is fun to make a multiplication matrix to show the children how many of the multiplication facts they have already mastered and how few there are to learn.

Obtain graph paper with squares big enough for the children to write a numeral in. I prefer 1/2 inch squares for most children. Cut out or draw a frame around an area with 12 x 12. Put a multiplication sign (x) in the top left square. Begin in the **next box** to the right and number each box from 1 to 11. Begin in the next box under the x and number each box from 1 to 11. Show the child how to move down from one numeral and across from another numeral to find the empty box that belongs only to

Practical Helps

those two numbers and write in the answer to the multiplication problem when they are multiplied together. (Down from 2 and across from 3 you will write 6, down from 5 and across from 4 you will write 20, and so on.) Have them fill in the ones they know quickly and easily. You will then know the ones you still need to teach and they need to practice.

Again make triangle flash cards. With 12 in the top corner, a multiplication sign in the middle and 3 and 4 in the lower corners, you can do four problems: 3x4=12, 4x3=12, 12 divided by 4=3, and 12 divided by 3=4

Divide

If you have used the triangle flash cards in the previous section, teaching division facts will be much easier than if you are coming at the topic cold. Even so, it is important that your children **see** what division is. A fun way to tackle this is through party treats. Have a party or pretend one. Have several different kinds of treats. Have several plates. Talk about each problem first, using the words divide, divided by, and divide into. Then show it by putting the treat on the plates and write the problem out. For example, make cupcakes. If you have a dozen cupcakes and 6 party guests, how many will each guest have? If only 3 people share those same dozen cupcakes, how many would they get? If you have a dozen cupcakes and a dozen guests, how many will each guest receive? If you have 15 toys and 3 party guests, how many toys will each guest get? After math class is over, eat the treats and keep the toys for a winning and memorable introduction to division.

➡️ **Timeless Teaching Tips**

About Rewards

To Reward or Not to Reward?

Rewards can be a topic of controversy. Let's think about it for a moment. If we bake a cake for our child's birthday, why do we do it? Because it reinforces our concept of who we are. Because we anticipate the child's delight when he sees (and tastes!) it. We don't just do it for no reason. We all work for rewards. Adults often work for intangible rewards. Children, especially young ones, need things they can see and feel and touch. Even the Bible suggests the use of rewards: God punishes evil, but He rewards obedience.

Make the reward fit the amount of effort necessary to earn it. Don't give an M & M for a month's work at learning a skill, controlling behavior, or practicing a good habit. On the other hand don't give a popcorn party or a trip for five minutes of attention to homework unless it was a long time coming! Sometimes use the reward as a carrot in front of the child where he has to carefully and deliberately earn it. Don't reward **every**

Practical Helps

moment and episode of compliance or you will develop a child who only works for rewards.

Let the child know what he must do to earn the reward, how often and for how long he must do it. Then keep a chart to record his efforts and progress. Occasionally give your child a reward, just because you love him - and tell him that is why you are giving it. Don't inundate his world with physical representations of your love (toys, clothes, books, etc.) and then withhold your own presence and attention.

Possible Rewards
Trip to: park, museum, restaurant, friends, etc.
Free time
Cars, dolls, coins, stamps, etc., to add to a collection. If he
 doesn't have one, encourage and help him to start one.
1/2 hour video or video game time
Food treat like taffy apple, ice cream, nuts, raisins, cookies
Popcorn party
Friend visit
Overnight guest
Time with parent to work on a special project like: build a tree-
 house or doll-house, ride bikes, go fishing, shopping, or
 swimming
Mini-golf
Money toward new sports equipment
Stickers
New toy
Milk shake
Fruit shake (blender ice cubes with banana and orange juice or
 strawberries, etc.)
New book of child's choosing

➡ Timeless Teaching Tips

Sports Equipment
Computer time
Cooking lesson
Carpenter tools and/or lesson
Gymnastic lessons
Swim time at the local Y
New clothes
"Date" with opposite sex parent
New pet or toy for pet

Don't let rewards control your life or your relationship with your children, but use them judiciously to benefit both.

Practical Helps

Including Young Children in the Homeschool

What do I do with the little ones? So many are asking that question and not coming up with answers! I frequently see two extremes, both of which result in some pretty dire consequences. One extreme is that the little ones are left on their own as long as they are not endangering themselves or others. That results in children who, at age five or six, are unprepared to be corralled into structured learning and submissive obedience when the concept of "school" is finally introduced. The opposite, and equally destructive, approach is to sit the two or three-year-old down at a desk with a paper and pencil and expect him to "do school" just like the older kids. That often results in burn-out by age 8 to 10 - just when the child should **really** be ready to devote himself to academic learning. A better approach, I think is to include the little ones in small doses of age and development appropriate structured learning opportunities from early ages on. God created us to be learners and every person is capable and ready to learn something every day of his life. The job of a true educator is to determine what

⇨ Timeless Teaching Tips

they are ready to learn and in what way it should be introduced and taught for the most meaningful learning. Little ones need to be included in "real life" activities whenever possible - and they are ready for some sit-down learning in small doses. There are also many learning activities that these little ones can do independently.

Include Your Young Ones!

Whenever possible, include the young ones in whatever you are doing. If you are cooking, give them their own containers and spoons and a bit of the batter. If you are cleaning, give them a dust rag or miniature broom. When you garden, give them a hand shovel, a bucket of soil, and a few seeds. When you fold laundry, teach them to fold the washclothes, napkins, and under ware and to sort by color, size, or owner. They like being close to you and enjoy being a part of whatever you are doing.

Clean up should include even the young children. Somewhere between the first and second birthday, little ones can be trained to "put it in the trash," "stack them neatly," "put the books on the shelf," "put all the toys in this container." If you have an organization plan that includes shelves, cupboards and containers for everything, the children can cooperate in keeping things in order. They will actually like it when they can find just the toy or book they want because they know where it is. You can make it easier for them by labeling shelves, cupboards and containers with picture labels. Sing a favorite song when it is time to clean up, put on some bouncy music, or appoint one child each day to musically entertain while the rest clean up. Make it fun, but not optional, that everyone pick up and put

Practical Helps

things away together. This should be done every day, preferably just before dad comes home. It is a great way to build good habits and attitudes toward having a house in order as well as please a very important person!

Laundry is a major part of any large household and should involve the entire family. Even infants enjoy the warm feel of a towel or washcloth fresh out of the dryer and the wonderful smell of laundry brought in from the line. Toddlers can "pull out all the socks," or "pull out all the wash-clothes" - or baby clothes or their own clothes. Preschoolers can sort the socks (first by size, then by color) and sort towels by size and clothes by whose they are. Preschoolers can also fold wash-clothes, kitchen and hand towels and smaller pieces of underwear. Older ones should learn to fold socks, underwear and towels to your specifications and to put their own clothes away properly. If drawers or closet space are too hard for your younger children, or inadequate in space, keep each child's clothing in containers. Use one container for underwear, one for tops, and one for skirts and pants. Hang only suits, dresses and Sunday best. If organization of clothes is a real problem, maybe you just have too many. Reduce clutter by cutting down on the number of clothes and toys, but **never** get rid of good books. Pass them down to the next generation!

I have discovered that when the little ones get a sufficient amount of attention for a while, they are happy and willing to go off and play by themselves if they have play materials that are appropriate and appealing. One way to increase appeal of their play-alone toys is to have five (to seven) large containers filled with toys which are only available one day a week. Each day put away the "daily toys" before supper or bedtime. The

⇨ Timeless Teaching Tips

next morning bring out a container that the children have not seen for a week. It will keep them busier than toys which they see every day. These containers can contain such things as puzzles, stacking and sorting toys, peel and stick letters or story telling characters, dress-up clothes, dolls with Velcro™ clothes, and trucks with a drawn road scene. You may want to give each container a different theme or color scheme. Coordinate the containers with other things you are teaching the little ones. The important thing is that they be full of interesting, sturdy objects that the children can use independently. You may want to make a list (in words, silhouettes or pictures) of what goes into each container to ease the-end-of-the-day clean up. Tape it inside the lid so they can find it when they need it.

Little ones catch more than you ever thought possible. They may be playing and apparently ignoring you completely, but

More is Caught than Taught.

they are hearing and learning. When you are going about household tasks, they notice attitudes. They learn to be disgusted, tired, sporadic workers - or cheerful, diligent at work and play. While you are teaching older ones, the little ones are also catching attitudes about learning - whether it is important, real, fun, exciting, interesting and something to look forward to or something which is boring, hateful, and tense to be avoided whenever possible.

An ideal situation for home schooling when there are little ones in the house is to have two adjoining rooms set aside for school. One can be arranged for the older ones, the other for the younger children. Mom's chair, desk, or table should be near the door that joins the two rooms so that she can see into both rooms.

Practical Helps

The little people's room should be child-proofed and include toys, dress-up clothes, comfy furniture, and a bathroom (or at least a potty chair and hand wipes) whenever possible. Their room should not have access to the outdoors or the rest of the house without an older person's help. The older children who are more easily distracted should be positioned as far as possible from the junction of the two rooms. When Mom is needed elsewhere, a responsible older sibling can be appointed to work near the little ones.

Make rules about the presence of the little ones in any room where intense

Make Simple Rules.

learning is taking place. They should be quiet (probably limited talking and only quiet play). They need to learn to interrupt politely (stand quietly with a hand on Mom or teacher). They should not interrupt unnecessarily (good practice for other situations). They may participate, ask relevant questions, give positive attention, leave to go to the restroom. They may stay in the area only as long as they are obeying these rules. Their stays (except for the rare happy quiet child) should be short (usually less than a half hour) and interspersed with active times outdoors or in another room where talking and large movements are permissible. This can be supervised by an older child.

"School" for the little ones should be little times of supervised activities. These times can usually come when the child is looking for attention, but occasionally take them from something they are enjoying so that they become used to dropping their play and responding to you. Some things which are good for this supervised time are painting and play dough, measuring and pouring dry grains, putting toys away, singing, snipping with a

⇨ Timeless Teaching Tips

blunt scissors, spreading a soft spread on toast or small cracker, reading a book together, making a simple craft, or taking a walk. Provide opportunity for supervised jumping and rolling on a trampoline, mini-tramp, or even an old couch or chair." Writing," "coloring" and "drawing" are important, but keep the sessions short and be willing to stretch the definition of the words and vary the materials. Children can "write" in the sand or in the air, draw in a piece of pie dough, and color with chalk, pencils or markers. Sorting and classifying by size, color, shape, and use are essential and can accompany such mundane tasks as putting groceries away and sorting laundry.

When you are making the schedule for the learning of your older ones, remember the little ones. Schedule yourself to be with them for 15 to 30 minute periods two or three times a day. Some of the older learners can also take their turns being scheduled to read them a story or take a walk or just play with the little ones. At meals, naps and bath time make sure they get a little attention again. Be sure to read to them at least once a day. And don't forget the importance of just a little talk. Ask them (perhaps at supper) what they did that was fun, what they had for lunch, or what they played with today. Dad can give them a few minutes, too, between supper and bed for reading aloud, listening, or play the audience for show and tell by looking at what they have made.

Reading aloud should stretch from the womb to the tomb. Being read to is soothing and comfortable for most children. Especially when begun from infancy, it builds skills in attention, listening, visual focus, vocabulary, and verbal language. It also begins a lifelong love for the sound of words, the importance of bonding, and, when well done, an appreciation for fine literature. The

Practical Helps

Bible and picture books are good places to start. Other wonderful sources for read aloud material include riddles and jokes, poetry, magazines, family photo albums, siblings' writings and letters from friends and families. Don't forget the child's baby book. If you don't have time to make one yourself, assign the job to an older sibling, a grandparent, godparent, or a loving, interested couple or single who would appreciate being included in the life of your family.

Many small children (and some older ones) cannot "sit **and** listen." Either takes all of their attention.

What can I DO While I Listen?

When it is time to listen, allow them to play with puzzles, blocks, dolls, books, color or draw. Other quiet and "mindless" activities may be encouraged. When they must really sit still, give them something to manipulate with their hands: a strong latex balloon filled with flour or rice, sports exercise putty or clay, any finger or hand exercise toy (check with medical suppliers for exercisers meant for people with arthritis), a doll or rubber bendable figure. If their hands have something to do, their mind is freed to listen. Food to nibble on or gum to chew is another option. Save gum or suck candy for the listening times. Then when you call them to listen, say, "It is time to listen. You may have your gum (wiggle toy, blocks, etc.) while you listen to this story." Suddenly they will be eager to come and listen!

Young children may stack blocks or line them up in a row. They can drive cars on a printed road, dress

Appropriate Activities for Little Ones.

and undress dolls, sort buttons, toys, or other small objects,

Timeless Teaching Tips

pour and fill containers (developing small muscle coordination). They can scribble, draw, paint, or write. They may match, sort, count, build, put away, or categorize (building coordination and thinking skills). These activities may be related to learning names of shapes, colors, and actions, counting, numerals, alphabet, alphabetical order, colors, animal names, animal babies, foods and categorizing (like in/out, up/down, liquids/solids, tall/short, vegetable/fruit, under/over farm/zoo, and so on). Provide many opportunities to listen to songs and stories, to run, play ball, and exercise on bikes, swings, and other equipment.

Quiet Activities.

Some good activities which involve a child quietly for a long time are: dressing dolls, sorting books or toys, dominoes, and puzzles, pouring and measuring grains, building with construction toys or blocks, screwing caps onto bottles or nuts onto bolts, using a snap-back tape measure, listening to an audio tape with a headset, filling jars with cotton balls, cotton swabs, or clothespins. Use your imagination! The more the job can be like the real work, the better the long-term benefit.

Make Simple Learning Games.

You don't need to spend a lot of money on games for children. Make some simple learning materials. The older children will enjoy helping. 3" x 5" file cards are invaluable to create all sorts of games. Cut them in half (2 1/2" x 3"). This size card stores nicely in a 2-pound processed cheese box. Make sets of cards for sorting, matching or playing concentration. Use stickers to make 10 sets of four matching cards to play "go fish" or "old maid." Print the capital letters in black on one set and lower case

Practical Helps

letters in red on another and have the child match the capital and lower case Aa, Bb, etc. Make two copies of each of ten words and have the child match them. Put a varying number of x's on each card and have the child put them in order. Or have him place one button or marker on each x. Then count them out loud with the child. Collect twigs. Break some into segments; make ten pieces of different lengths. Have the child organize them from shortest to longest. Have another bag with four each of five different lengths. Have them sort them into sets of four. Put self-sticking stickers on milk caps to make sets to sort.

Limit Artificial Life!

I can't leave the topic of young children without a word of caution. Years ago young children crawled and played and naturally developed perception and skills which were useful for their futures. Today too many children spend hours of their formative years in front of a screen - television, computers and computerized games. Their eyes do not develop the kind of perception needed in real life. Their hands do not coordinate well. They are unprepared for real-life relationships that demand polite, appropriate responses. Because the screen in front of them changes every few seconds, they do not develop a strong attention span. When they are old enough for school tasks, they are not developmentally ready. They are labeled attention deficit, learning disabled, slow learners, developmentally disabled... The list goes on and on. This is not the only cause of the problem, but I do believe it is an important factor in the huge increase of children who do not succeed in school tasks. Please, limit and supervise your child's time in these artificial worlds!

⇨ Timeless Teaching Tips

Watching and Helping Younger Siblings is Part of Learning.

When you need to work alone or with one of the older children, assign an older child to the younger one(s). This is a natural part of their developmental learning as well. They may play with them, read to them, or supervise structured activities or they may just be near by while doing their own work. Keep them near you if the "older child" is not very responsible - or send them downstairs or outdoors if he is.

Include Your Little Ones.

What specific activities you provide for your child to do is not nearly as important as making him feel included and a part of your world. He will develop skills as he has fun right at your feet and you are getting him ready to be a willing learner and worker as an adult. Home schooling is a challenge, but a rewarding one. The little ones are a part of the family and a part of the education of the older siblings. They are assimilating your attitudes toward small people and figuring out which you consider more important, academic subjects or real life learning. Don't neglect either. Find a comfortable, efficient, and enjoyable balance.

Homeschooling Issues

Happy Helpful Hints	161
Get a Jump Start!	167
MultiLevel Can be Fun and Easy!	170

Homeschooling Issues

Happy Helpful Hints

Here are some helpful hints guaranteed to make your day go easier.

Happiness is a major ingredient of learning. Children who enjoy the lesson retain more usable information. Children enjoy: bright

Happiness is Essential

colors, variety, music, pretend, miniatures, larger than life, creating and making things, jokes, silliness, movement, rhymes and rhythm, acting, and doing. Be sure to include large doses of these very important elements in your child's day. If education is not enjoyable, learning will probably be put on hold on graduation day.

Many new teachers err with classes that are too long. Just as children

Ten Minutes a Day

cannot eat a steak in one bite, they cannot master skills in huge chunks. Any *skill* that requires much repetition and practice for success is best done in tiny, frequent practice sessions. Skills

⇨ Timeless Teaching Tips

include things like learning to read, memorizing math facts, learning to roller blade, writing a report, playing a piano, learning a new language, memorizing terms and their definitions, etc. Ten minutes a day is often enough. A half an hour broken into smaller segments with variety and fun - may be ideal. Just think of the piano teacher who asks you to repeat a song three times in a row and practice one-half hour a day. Transfer her method to any skill you want your child to master.

Great Chunks of Information

On the other hand, **information can be assimilated** in great chunks if it is presented within a context and in a fun, multi-sensory way. Immersion in a subject is a good way to take in many facts at once. The more interrelated this information is the better. Pick a topic. Get some picture books, a game or two, a video, a few puzzles, science experiments, workbook pages, a biography or two, textbooks at several grade levels which cover the topic, and a novel on that subject. Every afternoon for a week spend an hour or two reading, playing, and working with that subject. Think of a field trip or project that extends the concepts you are developing. Devote a day to that project or field trip. Then give your family a chance to report to an audience in a novel way: make scrapbooks, create a newsletter, write and perform a play, dress in period costumes, write and present poems of songs, make mini-books or bigger-than-ever books. You will be amazed at how much your children learn! You may find yourself learning, too! And you may find it so much fun that you gradually slip into this "unit study" method of teaching for most of your time and subjects.

Homeschooling Issues

Mainstreaming children who have learning disabilities is not a service! For most children who learn differently, it means years of punishment, alienation, misunderstanding, frustration, and unfortunately, non-learning. Even worse - they may be learning, but not what you hoped. They may be learning inappropriate and avoidance behaviors. Mainstreaming means requiring the children who learn differently to do the same thing in the same way on the same time schedule as "average" learners. In order to thrive, they need changes in structure, variety in presentation, flexibility in requirements, and gentle direction.

> **Mainstreaming Is Painful!**

We are all different. Schools are geared toward academics, language, symbols, logic, sequence, and writing - all areas of frustration and stress for people who excel in big picture, relationships, arts and music, design, creativity, and other unique ways of looking at things.

People who learn differently need more space (physical and emotional) and more time to learn the same information. They need time to assimilate knowledge after it has been introduced. They must practice and play with concepts before they are mastered. Forcing them through a normal textbook curriculum at the average pace may stilt and frustrate intellectual growth and creative development.

Grammar comes later. Only some very basic grammar concepts need be formally taught before the fourth grade. This includes: a sentence begins with a capital and ends with a period, comma in a date, colon in

> **Wait for Grammar**

⇨ Timeless Teaching Tips

clock time, capital for names, and capitalize the little word I. Parts of speech are not usually taught till fourth grade or after. Unfortunately, they're seldom **taught** at all; they're introduced and then tested or reviewed.

| Teach Me to Read in Syllables |

Reading Syllables - Many children have difficulty learning to read words of two or more syllables even after they have mastered the shorter words. Build on the skill they have - reading short one-syllable words. Break the bigger word down into syllables. Make a card long enough to fold into syllables. For instance, it takes a card 2" x 3" for a word of one short syllable. If the word you want him to read has three syllables, make a card 2" x 9." Fold it into three segments of three inches each. Open the card out and print one syllable neatly on each segment. Accordion-fold it so that each syllable can be revealed separately. Start with words of two syllables. Show one syllable. If the child does not say it readily, say it for him. Then show **only** the next syllable. If the child does not say it quickly, say it for him. Continue to the end of the word through each syllable in this way and then go back to the first syllable. As quickly as he reads it, show the next. Then show both syllables and say the word. Any time he does not respond as quickly as he would if reading a single syllable word, read it for him. If this still seems difficult, read each syllable with him. Begin with words that have syllables that are real words, like napkin and cabinet. As those are mastered, try words with syllables that are not real words, but easy to pronounce like hos-pit-al-it-y and co-op-er-ate.

Homeschooling Issues

Breaking Things Down into Smaller Steps - This is a general statement akin

> **Break it into Steps**

to the previous one. If your student is failing day after day, it may be the fault of the person who is designing his work! Every person can succeed if he is given work within his ability. Tiny steps of progress combined with consistent practice build confidence and success. If your child can't succeed at what you are asking of him, break it down, practice frequently in short stints, and watch success and joy happen!

Success Ends Failure - 90% of the time the only thing needed to turn failure to achievement is success. All children need success every day. (So do adults!) It is not enough to have success in math and struggle

> **Success Ends Failure**

in reading; learners need success in every subject they tackle on a given day. If they are struggling with no success at all, they will give up. Break tasks down to small achievable steps and back up until your student finds success. Then move forward gradually in tiny steps.

Picture Books Introduce - many non-fiction picture books include as much information as is needed on a subject through fourth grade level.

> **All Ages Love Picture Books**

They are also excellent for giving the big picture that is the best way to introduce a new or difficult concept. I often use children's non-fiction to begin researching a new topic I plan to write about. They help me skim the surface, point out the most important concepts and show the whole topic in a short sitting.

⇨ Timeless Teaching Tips

Then I fill in what needs more thorough study. Use the same idea with all ages; then have each one choose a facet of the subject to study in more depth.

Memorizing Scripture Builds Skill

Reciting Scripture Builds Character, Memorization, and Other Skills - During the optimum language acquisition stage (up till about six), inundate the child with Scriptures. It will be easy for him to memorize frequently repeated language and it will build memorization skills effortlessly. (It won't hurt your older learners either!) Read or recite one scripture at breakfast, another at lunch, and a different one at dinner (and other strategic times during the day such as naptime, bedtime, etc.). Repeat the same scriptures daily. After a month, change the scriptures. Review for one month each year.

Believe in Me!

Believe in Your Child and His Ability to Become - I can't stress enough the importance of this! Every person was created for success and improvement. When no one cares...when no one challenges...when no one tries...**then** no one succeeds! We need each other. If you want a job that lasts a lifetime and has abundant rewards, find the down-and-outer and love and encourage him! When he succeeds, you succeed with him. Unfortunately some adults have become so comfortable in failure that they are well-rooted, but children are just waiting for that encourager who will support them! Be your child's encourager and bond him to yourself for life!

Homeschooling Issues

Get a Jump Start!

Has your child just stopped making progress? Perhaps he or she has hit a plateau or has been diagnosed "learning disabled." Here are a few pointers:

Look back to how you were teaching when they were learning. Perhaps it

> **How did they learn?**

was when they were two or three and you made everything a game. Or a time when they were allowed to show what they knew by drawing a picture or acting it out or doing a project. Maybe it was when you were teaching them something *they really wanted to know.* Or it was when you were more rested and really enjoyed what you were doing? When you think of that time, try to recapture it in miniature to give yourself a jump start back into the world of learning. Whatever you did then, try it again. Whether it was attitude, technique, or materials use what was successful and start over.

⇨ **Timeless Teaching Tips**

Take a break. Use this time to take a break from normal academics and a time to concentrate on other ways of learning. Take a few major field trips perhaps related to what you were trying to teach. Teach the skills involved in playing board games while you teach proper sportsmanship in winning and losing. (There are many board games related to various subjects of history and science.) Make a new friend as you minister to someone through nursing home or hospital visitation. Develop new skills in carpentry, painting, or some other hobby. Record what you are doing in a notebook. Include photos, narrative, samples of work, labeling of charts and diagrams, momentos and keepsakes.

Eliminate one subject. A variation of number two is to eliminate the one specific subject, topic or concept that is giving difficulty for a limited time while you think of new ways to approach it and give your child time to mature and assimilate what he has heard with no pressure. If it's math in general, switch to math tricks, games and practical uses, like banking, measuring, cooking, or using a calculator. Avoid traditional math pages for a while. When you resume, do so slowly, doing only half a page at a time or requiring only every other problem.

Let someone else try. If the problem seems to be only in one subject, find someone else who might try to teach it in an entirely new way - perhaps your husband, an aunt, and older

Homeschooling Issues

child, or a good friend. Sometimes it only takes a slightly different approach to make the whole thing seem easy!

Back off the pressure, and come at the problem area from the back door. Don't worry so much about whether the child is "getting it," but make it a point to talk about the concept frequently. Show its truth in as many ways as possible. Make the difficult concept a friendly part of your life. Before long you'll find that the child has grasped it naturally.

Don't pressure!

Most important, pray for your child and your job as a home educator! Have fun and enjoy learning and teaching your child. That will make it easier for you both!!

⇨ **Timeless Teaching Tips**

MultiLevel Can Be Fun and Easy!

Ripples are out there. Ripples of discontent and fear and wonder and excitement. Some homeschooling moms who have been staunchly in favor of one particular textbook curriculum or another are getting the seven-year itch. They are hearing things. They are wondering if maybe there is something to this unit study stuff after all. But it is so foreign! So unstructured! So open! Will it fit those who have been so comfortable with the familiar?

Though the whole idea of multilevel teaching is intimidating to many parents who homeschool, it needn't be. It is really easier in the end than juggling several stacks of grade level texts. It also allows each child to absorb as much as he is truly ready for regardless of grade level limitations, therefore both the gifted and the learning challenged find themselves more comfortable and learning more readily than in age or grade dependent curricula. It does require some adjustment in thinking and preparation,

Homeschooling Issues

especially for the parent/teacher, because we have spent so many years seeing only one example of how to teach. Here are some suggestions on how to sneak in gently.

Don't chuck everything that is familiar and comfortable and switch completely and fully to something new and strange. When you buy a new pair of shoes, you are not likely to throw out all the old ones and start from the first day wearing only the new. At first give unit study or the multi-level approach a little trial. One day a week, one week a month or one month a year, try it on for size. Like those new shoes, it may pinch a bit at first, but be willing to keep at it a little at a time for a while and see if an adjustment is possible. Promise yourself you will try again. Don't throw out the old ways completely until the new ways are broken in and comfortable.

Try it Out Slowly.

Unit study doesn't have to be formidable. It may be as simple as this: Pick a topic all your children might be interested in like middle ages, the human body, or butterflies. Read a book to the whole group. Picture books are a great way to start! Then go to a related article in an encyclopedia. Share what you find. Notice the outline and related articles at the end. Think of an activity of some kind that goes with the topic. This may be dressing up, writing a play, skit, song, or poem, making something, going somewhere, or drawing and labeling a picture, chart or graph. If you have access to texts or workbooks, see if there is a related chapter for the children to do. Puzzles, games, crosswords, coloring books, biographies, and science experiments are all ways to enhance the

Start Simply.

⇨ Timeless Teaching Tips

learning. Finally come together to share what you've been doing. It is that easy!

It is important to discover the benefits and blessings of picture books. When I begin to research a new topic, I start in the children's section of the library and check out several related picture books. Most well written non-fiction picture books cover the topic fairly well up through the third or fourth grade level. They also provide an excellent introduction and show the big picture for those of us who can't figure out what to do with the many details until we are familiar with the whole. Read each book aloud. This entertains and informs the little ones at their level while it provides good examples of meaningful reading with expression for the older ones. Since younger children love repetition, have the older ones read the best books again and again, reviewing and refreshing their understanding of the topic as they practice oral reading skills. Make note of any details that interest or confuse any of the children. These may be areas for more in-depth studies.

Next, go to the youth section of the library and find other books related to the topic. Let the older children scan them and share any information they find interesting or important. Suggest that they be thinking of a project they and/or the little ones might enjoy being involved in. Encourage informal sharing as well as the more formal oral and written reports. If there is an *EyeWitness, Living History, Time Traveler* or *Kingfisher* book on the topic, it will enhance the study nicely and all ages will enjoy the pictures. Get out the encyclopedias and spend an hour or two looking up related ideas and sharing, conversation-style, what you find. If you have stacks of textbooks, encourage the readers to use them like an encyclopedia and dig for new

Homeschooling Issues

information, interesting pictures, charts, or maps and pertinent facts. Check the table of contents, index and glossaries for pertinent information.

Meanwhile, note the people involved in discovery and development of the topic and get some biographies. Each of the older children could read one individually. Choose one to read aloud to the family. Choose carefully, but don't limit the reading level of the biography. Sometimes the picture book level biographies like the *Step Up Biographies* or Jean Fritz's books are delightful and informative. On the other hand, another children's series that is widely available eliminates all mention of church, God or spiritual influences on the decisions of the people in history. This can be misleading and subtly dangerous. Don't neglect historical fiction, but again be cautious of the perspective of the author. Books like *Adam of the Road, Bronze Bow,* and *Least of All* can add tremendously to your understanding.

Get the librarian involved. Ask her to help you find a few books and/or videos on the subject. Tell her you'd like books relevant to your topic on different levels - like picture books, nonfiction juvenile, biographies, and even magazine or encyclopedia articles. Give her a warning of a week or two and you may be surprised at what she can find. Meanwhile, comb your favorite supplier's catalog for a game, coloring book, or activity book related to the topic. Check out the Internet. Ask input from friends and relatives. Sometimes an aunt or an elderly friend would love to have something to do and will be on the alert for games or newspaper articles on your topic. Maybe grandfather could help the children build something related to the topic.

⇨ Timeless Teaching Tips

Then, when the afternoon or week arrives, start off by reading one or more picture books to the whole family. Open a discussion. Make a list of all the things the family already knows about the topic. Make another list of questions they'd like answered. Add your own thoughts as appropriate. Begin to read a biography aloud. Play the game or give the young ones a picture to color. By now, each child needs an assignment. It may be to read a book, search for the answer to one of the questions, or build a model with blocks or clay. It may be to draw and label a picture, write a story, or research a complex idea. It may be to trace the topic through history, or find the topic in the Bible, or make a list of all the famous people who had anything to do with the topic. The children may help determine their own assignment or offer to find out something.

Give them Time!

Give them some time with the books you've collected. The youngest ones will probably be most interested in the pictures. Middle ones may read the captions to them. The older ones may need another trip to the library to find out more information now that they have some idea what the topic covers. Every day play the game for a while, and read a little from the biography. If possible, take a field trip or do a group project related to the topic. Then assist each child in having something to share with the group. Give them a time to show and share. Before you consider yourselves done, go back to your list of what they "knew" and what they wanted to learn. Was their "knowledge" accurate? See if you can now answer some of the questions. List any unanswered questions and assign someone to research them. Make a new list of things that you learned. Encourage everyone to list at least one new idea. Make a chart or graph of the new ideas.

Homeschooling Issues

Now the fun really begins! If the children have thought of projects, assist in obtaining the needed materials as necessary, but encourage them to delve in on their own with older children assisting younger ones. Obtain at least one coloring book, game, or project book (like Usborne cutout models or Science in a Nutshell) on the topic. They give hands-on learners a chance to shine and enhance the retention of all. Music, such as *Wee Sing* and Diana Waring's *Westward Ho!*, also bring life to the topic, aid memory, and include auditory learners. Give the children at least a week at this point of the study to get really involved. If any seem "stuck," meet with them individually or pair them with another who needs help. Plan a field trip to a museum when appropriate.

Older learners may need deeper involvement and a specific assignment. Here is where I turn to a good encyclopedia. I prefer *World Book* in general and the older, the better, for most topics! I look up the topic myself and check out the outline and related topics. For instance, when studying worms, I noted immediately that there were four types of worms. The high schooler's assignment? Write a report on the four types of worms; include at least three references. I was off the hook until I had to read and evaluate his paper.

As the study draws near the end (studies can last from a week to a year), plan to provide an audience

Show and Share!

for sharing what they've learned and made. Each child should share his own reports, drawings, and projects. Each one should prepare something to show and something to tell. And you thought "show and tell" was for kindergarten! Dad,

➪ Timeless Teaching Tips

grandparents and close friends are obvious as potential guests, but don't neglect others. If you have a relative or neighbor who is antagonistic toward homeschooling, or just doesn't understand the concept, now is the time to win them over. Or invite the children's public school friends. Include an older couple who have no children or a live-alone. Plan an evening to include dinner and a "show." Make invitations to send or have one child phone. If the night you have chosen isn't convenient for them, be flexible. Invite the whole family. Include your children in the food preparation. Make foods appropriate for the period you are studying. Take pictures of the event. Include a song or two - preferably at least one that even the guests will know. Have a wonderful time!

Throughout the process, take many pictures. Snap the children as they listen, read, play, and work. When the pictures are developed (make at least two prints of each, more if you have a big family), let each child choose a few. Have them write a sentence or paragraph about what was happening. Put them into a scrapbook or a poster. Or make two books and give one to the "audience" as a remembrance. The more you can take the study back into real life, the better. Best of all, they'll have learned in a real setting which encourages them to understand that learning is a natural part of life - not something to be endured for the school years.

Multilevel teaching? Multilevel learning! If everyone involved doesn't learn something new in most of these studies, I don't know people. For, you see, God blesses homeschooling for many reasons, but one of them is that this is His way of educating two generations at once. The parents who today are homeschooling are, for the most part, a product of the public

Homeschooling Issues

school system. We have so much to unlearn and had so little time to truly learn that it may be hard to keep up with our kids! Multilevel teaching is a fun way to begin. Try it a few times, and you just might find yourself giving more and more attention to this new way and less and less to the textbook-assignment-for-every-subject-every-day-for-every-child method. If the shoe fits, wear it!

⇨ Timeless Teaching Tips

Gems

Children	179
Learning Differences	193
Teaching	197
Parents	210
Training Character	213
Christian Training	215
School	221

 *Gems*

Children

A Child

...wants to learn...
...wants to explore...
...wants to please...
...needs success...
...seeks meaning...
...responds naturally...
...looks for answers...
...asks for help...

Children are natural followers.
They are watching and absorbing
everything that goes on around them.

Children see attitudes and motives that they cannot verbalize. They understand the heart, even when they don't understand the words.

 **Timeless Teaching Tips**

☆☆☆☆☆☆☆☆☆☆☆☆☆☆☆☆☆☆☆☆☆☆☆

Children appreciate most the gift of our time.

Problem is,
if we never have it when they are small,
they outgrow the desire to share it with us.

One day this week, let the dishes wait
ignore the dirt piling up, leave the laundry
undone, put the answering device on...

and take the children on a mini-vacation:
  a trip to the zoo, a picnic in the park,
  a boat ride, a day at the beach...

What you do isn't as important as spending
uninterrupted, unscheduled time together
doing something you all enjoy.

When they are grown, these impromptu moments
are the times they will remember
and tell you that they loved.

Children naturally mimic those they respect, admire and enjoy.

<<<<<<<<<<<<<<<<<<<<<<<<<<<<<<<<<<<<<<

 *Gems*

❖ ❖

Children are becoming
what
they spend time with.

What are your children becoming?

XXXXXXXXXXXXXXXXXXXXXXXXXXXXXXXXXXXX

We protect our children

from storms

in the physical world.

Let's do the same spiritually.

✶✶✶✶✶✶✶✶✶✶✶✶✶✶✶✶✶✶✶✶✶✶✶✶✶✶✶✶✶✶✶✶✶✶✶✶

Show me. Tell me. Let me do it. Then I'll understand.

Run so you can win!

➡ Timeless Teaching Tips

XXXXXXXXXXXXXXXXXXXXXXXXXXXXXXXXXXXXXXXXXXX

Children can appear to learn something before they have really mastered it. You think they have it, but the next day they don't know what you are talking about. What is the answer?

    Constant review! They need to review things frequently and over a long period of time.

This review should be provided in many different ways - through games and plays, oral drill and highlighting information in books, writing summaries and teaching a friend. Children work better, learn faster, and retain more if the pace is fast and there is lots of variety. They enjoy being silly and laughing. They need to learn limits to silliness and will do that best at home. Don't worry if your child seems to need more repetition than you can believe. They enjoy and benefit from repetition!

There are great benefits to hearing the same information over and over in different ways, contexts and teaching styles. It sinks deep into our subconscious. It becomes part of us. It affects our lives.

Be sure that most of the things your children are hearing over and over are things that are worth being carried into the future!

 *Gems*

✓✓✓✓✓✓✓✓✓✓✓✓✓✓✓✓✓✓✓✓✓✓✓✓✓✓✓

You teach your child what you value
by what you praise.

Praise effort.
Praise success.

Praise worthy attitudes,
cheerfulness, and
compassion

Praise improvement.

Praise worthy character traits:
   diligence
   patience
     helpfulness

➡ Timeless Teaching Tips

<<<<<<<<<<<<<<<<<<<<<<<<<<<<<<<<<<<<<<<

When you were a child, did you spend as many hours playing board games with friends as I did?

What were you learning?

to cooperate with others	to take turns
to win graciously	to lose gracefully
to have fun in a group	to make choices
to appreciate friends	to count
to be involved with life	to read

to learn from mistakes
to think in sequence
to understand and use strategies
to deal with the consequences of choices
to stick with something until it is finished
to leave something unfinished when necessary

Give your children the same joys and benefits!
Give them time for board games.

<<<<<<<<<<<<<<<<<<<<<<<<<<>>>>>>>>>>>>>>>>>>>>>>

 *Gems*

Make a "Happiness is" List

List things you hear
or say
or do
that bring you or someone else
happiness.

Add to the list whenever you can.

When you are sad, read the list.
Then go and do or say
one of the things on the list.

When you make someone else happy,
it comes back to you.

Here is a start:
Sunlight and roses.
Eating spaghetti.
Watching children.
Planting a garden.

A chick which doesn't struggle from the egg is forever crippled.

 **Timeless Teaching Tips**

What children really want from us is time.
They spell love T-I-M-E.

Plan one day very soon
to spend a block of unstructured, unscheduled
time
with your children.

Go on a picnic.
Spend a day at the lake.
Hike in the mountains.
Visit the zoo.
Make a tent in the backyard and have lunch there.
Spend a rainy day reading books
and making cookies.
Get out the finger paints
and go to a table in the yard.
Spend all day in the back yard with the kids.
Get some dress-up clothes
and make up some skits.
Roast hot dogs outdoors over a fire.

What you do isn't as important
as that you take the time to enjoy
being **together.**

 *Gems*

m m m m m m m m m m m m m m m m m m m m m m

Children become what they live with daily.

Look around.

Try to see through the eyes of your neighbors -
through the eyes of your children.
What do you see in the home you have created?
What sounds do you hear?

What pictures, posters and banners are in your house?
What books and magazines sit on your shelves?
Who do you invite into your home through
television, radio, cassettes, and so on?

If you tally the minutes your children hear and
see the Word of God and other godly influences
against the minutes they hear and see
the things of the world -

which would win?

///

➡ Timeless Teaching Tips

!!!

Often people give more attention to the negative things children do than to the positive traits. Give praise often. Let your children know that you notice the good things they do. Call attention to traits and skills you want to see continue.

Things to Praise:
  Organization
  Clean up
  Helpfulness
  Cheerful obedience
  Attentive listening
  Cooperation
  Pleasant attitude
  Effort

Words of Praise:
  I'm impressed with the way you.....
  Thank you for.....
  You really surprised me when you...
  You're doing an incredible job!
  What would I do without you?
  I really appreciate it when you...
  You really made my day when...
  What a pleasure! What joy! Oh, happiness!

  How did you think of that great idea?

!!!

 *Gems*

Some children fare well with specific rules for tasks we consider obvious or simple.

List of rules for following instructions.

Read the first sentence.
Make sure you know the meaning of each word.
Ask the meaning of any words you do not understand.

Read the next sentence.
Do you know the meaning of each word?
Do you need help?

Read each sentence.
Make sure you know the meaning of each word.
Ask the meaning of any words you do not understand.

Read the instructions again.
Make sure you know the meaning of each sentence. Think again about the meaning of any part you may not understand.

Try to do the first step. Check it against the instructions. If it seems right, go on. If you still have questions, ask for help.

➪ Timeless Teaching Tips

(((((((((((((((((((((())))))))))))))))))))))

Set up a system of rewards and punishment.
God rewards obedience and punishes disobedience. We must do the same.
Little rewards should be built in to the day.
You could use tiny stickers.
When a child comes on time, does five math problems correctly, finishes an assignment, etc., he gets a sticker.
When he has earned twenty-five or fifty, there should be a reward (ten minutes of free time, a trip to a park or the mall, an ice cream cone, computer game time, etc.).
The child must know what he is expected to do and what happens if he fails to do it.

///

 *Gems*

Do you trust your child to make choices?
Even within a set framework,
there should be room for choices.

Do you allow him to make mistakes
and profit from them?

Do you allow him to ask questions and
encourage him to seek out his own answers?

Do you allow your child to be a person while you foster independence and responsibility, or are you too busy doing it all for him and thereby keeping him a helpless child?

➪ Timeless Teaching Tips

☞☞☞☞☞☞☞☞☞☞☞☞☞☞☞☞☞☞☞☞☞

There is a tendency among homeschooling families to try to do too much - to be too perfect - to make sure nothing is missed -
to concentrate too heavily on academics.

Remember your children are children.
They will never again be children.

Let them be children part of every day
so that they will not revert to childhood
as soon as they are free of restraints.

> A sixteen-year-old making up
> for a missed childhood
> will get into far more trouble
> than a five-year-old!

??????????????????????????????

 *Gems*

Learning Differences

++++++++++++++++++++++++++++++++++++++

If our society were more mechanically inclined, I would be labeled "mechanically disabled" and my husband would be a high achiever winning all kinds of awards.

~~~~~~

When academics and/or paying attention are a struggle, limit the time of struggle and reward paying attention this way:

Set a timer for twice as long as the assignment should take.

Let your student know that if he "Beats the Clock," he may have the remainder of the time to play.

When the assignment is done, and approved, give him the timer and note at what time it will ring.

He is to return to work when the timer rings.

Have his next assignment ready then.

Set the timer and start all over again.

⇨ **Timeless Teaching Tips**

★★★★★★★★★★★★★★★★★★★★★★★★

Disability, deficit, disorder: through a child's eyes all equal DUMB!

❖❖❖❖❖❖❖❖❖❖❖❖❖❖❖❖❖❖❖❖❖❖❖❖

Teach from the concrete to the abstract (in word pictures and parables).

jjjjjjjjjjjjjjjjjjjjjjjjjjjjjjjjjjjjjjjjjjjjjjjjjjjjjjjjjjjjjjjjjjjjjjj

As much as possible gear the amount of practice to the need of the learner.

✤✤✤✤✤✤✤✤✤✤✤✤✤✤✤✤✤✤✤✤✤✤✤✤

Gradually increase what you expect.

✺✺✺✺✺✺✺✺✺✺✺✺✺✺✺✺✺✺✺✺✺✺✺✺

Do not present programs; teach children.

 *Gems*

....

Everyone has talents and skills.

Everyone has needs.

Serving is knowing my talents and skills and giving them freely to your needs.

✓✓✓✓✓✓✓✓✓✓✓✓✓✓✓✓✓✓✓✓✓✓✓

Do not do for them what they can do for themselves,
unless time is of the essence.
They will learn that their efforts
are not appreciated or valuable.
Once learned, that is a stronghold not easily broken.

✱✱✱✱✱✱✱✱✱✱✱✱✱✱✱✱✱✱✱✱✱✱✱✱✱✱✱✱✱✱✱✱✱✱✱✱✱✱

**Students work better
when they understand what is wanted
and how well they are doing.**

✦✦✦✦✦✦✦✦✦✦✦✦✦✦✦✦✦✦✦✦✦✦✦✦✦✦✦✦✦✦✦✦✦✦✦✦✦✦

 **Timeless Teaching Tips**

Strengths of Children Who Learn Differently

They learn readily through music and rhythm.
They are often quite logical and precise
They know "everything there is to know"
about something they like.
They seek meaning.
They have very tender and sympathetic feelings
toward the underdog.
They are very artistic.
They are often creative.
They are very spiritually sensitive.
They seem to have a special hot line to heaven.

If these traits are encouraged and fed,
these people are capable of accomplishing much
in the kingdom of God!

Summarized from author's book
Learning in Spite of Labels

****

Praise small progresses.

****

We need 80% success to continue trying.

 *Gems*

Teaching

✢✢✢✢✢✢✢✢✢✢✢✢✢✢✢✢✢✢✢✢✢✢✢✢

Persistence is Learned

Have an on-going project
that each one in the family can work on together.

This should be something that takes
several months
or a year or more.

(A doll house, quilt, a back yard fort,
a soapbox car, garden, etc.)

Take pictures of the process.
Write stories about the process.

Celebrate when you finish!

++++++++++++++++++++++++++++++++++++

Preparation is necessary,
but should never rise above teaching.
Leave time for questions, creativity, and the Holy Spirit.

Capturing those learnable moments is essential.

◊ ◊ ◊ ◊ ◊ ◊ ◊ ◊ ◊ ◊ ◊ ◊ ◊ ◊ ◊ ◊ ◊

The good teacher encourages
God-given intelligence.

& & & & & & & & & & &

 **Timeless Teaching Tips**

ΩΩΩΩΩΩΩΩΩΩΩΩΩΩΩ

Are you reading aloud to your children?
If you choose wholesome biographies
to read to them,
you will be teaching them:

thinking
and listening skills,
history,
and correct grammar,

as you expose them to good literature,
and
develop their character.

Talk about easy lesson plans!

∧∧∧∧∧∧∧∧∧∧∧∧∧∧∧∧∧∧∧∧∧

**Teach the child to:
research
reason
relate
record**

 *Gems*

@@@@@@@@@@@@@@@@@@@@@@@

Good teachers depend on truth.

uuuuuuuuuuuuuuuuuuuuuuuuuuuuuuuuuuuuuuuuuuuuuuuu

Creative writing starters:

Today is...
I want to...
Yesterday, I...
Today we will...
I would like to learn about...
My family likes to...
I learned about...
One book I like is...
One thing that really makes me happy is...
One person that loves me is...
One thing I know about God is...
I know how to...
I would like to learn how to...
God is...
IF _____ THEN_____

uuuuuuuuuuuuuuuuuuuuuuuuuuuuuuuuuuuuuuuuuuuuuuuu

**Please,
teach children,**
not a curriculum.

,,,

Inspire from the heart out.

⇨ **Timeless Teaching Tips**

Show the way by going ahead (LEAD).

Make learning fun.
Make practice fun
for the learner.
Then they'll do it
without being forced.

Rank these twice: first in order of importance, then in order of time you spend on each:

Academics, Relationships, Skills

What does that say to you?

 *Gems*

Secrets of Teachers

What do you mean plan ahead?
       Sometimes we write the "plans" after the fact!

Follow teachable moments! When your student shows a spark of enthusiasm, take time to kindle the fire!

Don't feel a need to "cover a text!"

Choose the sequence by skimming the book and teaching the best and most important parts in the most teachable times.

December and June are not good teaching months - review!

January and October (and July in the deep south) are good months to hit the books.

Call your child whatever grade is appropriate,
       but let him work at his level of progress.

When the natives are restless, play a review game
       or assign calm quiet copying or reading.

Expect spurts of learning followed by plateaus or assimilation.

Keep a semi-scheduled life, but be prepared for interruptions. Capitalizing on interruptions is as important as planning well.

If they help plan, design or make it, they'll remember it longer.

Children are people first, learners second, and students third.

 **Timeless Teaching Tips**

♦♦♦♦♦♦♦♦♦♦♦♦♦♦♦♦♦♦♦♦♦♦♦♦♦♦♦♦♦

Transition from active to quiet classes by:

the example of your quiet, calm voice,

your slowed movements,

and your manner.

Tell them before they go to the area

what they will do

and in what manner they should do it.

vvvvvvvvvvvvvvvvvvvvvvvvvvvvvvvvvvvvvvvvvvvvvvvvvvvv

**Teach principles
and truths
that last forever,**

**not facts that
become obsolete
in a few years.**

ggggggggggggggggggggggggggggggggggggggggggggggggggggg

 *Gems*

Making plans?

Ask two questions:

What's the goal?

What's the strategy?

Or, put more simply,

What do you want to do?

How to you hope to accomplish it?

Don't let a curriculum or a textbook do your thinking.

Use it as a tool
to accomplish God's goals.

➡️ **Timeless Teaching Tips**

If you plan to succeed in homeschooling, it is very important that you organize your materials. Set aside a room that is prepared for schoolwork. Put in shelves or labeled cupboards or drawers. Your supplies must be at your fingertips to enhance your own creativity and make it easy for you to switch from one activity to the next. This does not have to look like a schoolroom with rows of desks. The dining room may work well if you are willing to have your materials stored there. If you have two adjacent rooms, one room could be fixed with toys and games for younger children. There might be a child-gate between them, then you could observe the little ones, but they would not be able to disturb the activities and projects of the your older learners. If you have older children, they may need a private study area in their own rooms away from the hustle and bustle of busy little ones. The important thing is to have a room ready for instant teaching and ongoing learning.

 *Gems*

To Teach Spelling

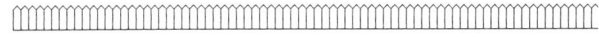

Teach principles,
not memorization of a list of words.

Teach application of principles in short words
and then in syllables of larger words.

Teach phonic principles first, then proceed with
a comprehensive spelling program.

Three words a day is better
than 30 words a week.
Choose words the child does not know.
Practice in a variety of ways until the child is
proficient.
The next day, review five old words before
studying three new ones.

Teach use of dictionary and/or computer
spelling checker.

 **Timeless Teaching Tips**

9999999999999999999999999999999

If you teach

addition of simple fractions

verbally first,

the paper work will be smoother.

"One-third plus one-third equals two-thirds," sounds right.

1/3 plus 1/3 = 2/3

doesn't look right

unless you understand what it means.

Education and learning **should** take diligence and work (on the part of the student!).

rtrtrtrtrtrtrtrtrtrtrtrtrtrtrtrtrtrtrtrtrtrtrtrtrtrtrtrtrtrtrtrtrtrtrtrtrtrtrtrtrtrtrt

Teach principles, not just facts.

 *Gems*

Secrets of Effective Teaching
First show what you mean.
Then explain it.
Show it again.

Do it with the learner.
Have the learner do it as you watch and give clues as necessary.

Then ask the learner to do it (without help),
explain it,
and do something with it.

That is real teaching
and brings about real learning.

Inspire the student to conquer.

➪ Timeless Teaching Tips

✱✱✱✱✱✱✱✱✱✱✱✱✱✱✱✱✱✱✱✱✱✱✱✱✱✱✱✱✱✱✱

Enhance successful learning with:

- Warm and helpful learning environment
- A great deal of encouragement
- Many successful experiences
- Relevant, hands-on presentation of concepts
- Rate of presentation geared to needs of student
- Hard work interspersed with easier and more fun activities
- A controlled level and amount of fun and silliness
- Adequate time to practice skills until mastery is proven

> The most important factor
> in successful learning
> is the teacher/student relationship!

To teach an unknown, relate it to a known.

> Do not teach what
> you will have to unteach.
> (Do not teach what you know
> will not be true in the future.)

Gems

Do not consider that you have taught
until
your student has learned,

or

you have (or he has) put it into a format
that will enable him to go back later
for review and re-teaching.

Do not concentrate on punishment.
Use only as much as necessary to bring about the desired effect. State what you expect and then expect it.

Do not teach the learner to look
for your approval only.
This teaches them to depend more on your approval than on themselves.

 **Timeless Teaching Tips**

Parents

Every parent

experiences the time

when a child looks up **at** them.

But each parent

must deliberately give their children cause

to look up **to** them.

The only thing that will stop you
is your own character flaws
which is exactly what God wants you to deal with.

There is a fine balance to walk on most issues.
Both extremes are usually harmful in the end.

 *Gems*

Redeem the Day

Some days go better than others.
It is important that even the "bad days" have
some good in them.

Find time at the end of a bad day
to redeem the day.

Every day try to have one family activity:
blow bubbles and giggle,
read a book under the tree,
romp with the dog,
eat popsickles in bed
while you listen to a story,
picnic in the shade.

Have a few wonderful moments together.

Then at supper, ask,
"What was your favorite part of today?"

Remember the good,
and forgive each other for the rest.

 **Timeless Teaching Tips**

When you say, "Go clean your room," did you ever wonder what that means to your child? Usually it means, "Move one thing to a new place."

Here is a great way to teach them what you mean!

Take your child to his own room. Spend whatever time necessary to straighten the room... working together with him. As you work, talk about where you are putting each thing and why you keep it there. When the room is very clean, take pictures of every small part, from the inside of drawers to the walls of the closet. Then post these pictures inside the closet door where they can be used like a checklist.

You may want to have order the jobs by priority. Or have a "once over lightly" job. When you send your child to his room to clean, tell him which picture he is to follow. Then he can see when his job is done.

> Now he knows exactly what you mean
> when you say, "Go clean your room!"

If he still does not do it, deal with his disobedience.

 *Gems*

Training Character

Little daily attitudes and habits have profound effects on future character.

///////////////////////////////////

Today is a good day to make a gift and take it to a shut-in. How about a book mark, a greeting card,
a picture or poster, a quilt,
a bouquet,
or a plate of cookies?

Perhaps you could plan to
read to them,
sing for them,
or have a question ready to ask,
or a story to tell.

Or maybe they just need a hug and a smile.
Visit a neighbor, call a friend,
or go to a nursing home.

Someone somewhere would appreciate your touch today.

 **Timeless Teaching Tips**

Be quick to listen,
careful to think and pray,
slow to answer.

Mistakes are a natural part of life
and an essential part of the learning process.
Allow mistakes.
Don't allow mistakes to be overwhelming.

If you value what he does,
he will know that you value who he is.

 *Gems*

Christian Training

We are called to walk in the good works Christ put in us.

▶ ▶ ▶ ▶ ▶ ▶ ▶ ▶ ▶ ▶ ▶ ◀ ◀ ◀ ◀ ◀ ◀ ◀ ◀ ◀

Can you balance this?
30 hours of secular education   1 hour of Sunday School
+ 40 hours of secular television,
toys and books

To learn, you must want to be taught.
Proverbs 12:1 The Living Bible

In the Bible we read that Timothy was taught
by his mother and grandmother
(he had unbelieving father).
Though this boy was raised primarily by females,
he became a strong man for the Lord.

MMMMMMMMMMMMMMMMMMMMMMMMMM

We must cultivate our children's
God-given capacity to see
every subject through Christ
and for Christ.

⇨ Timeless Teaching Tips

✤✤✤✤✤✤✤✤✤✤✤✤✤✤✤✤✤✤✤✤✤✤✤✤✤✤✤✤

A simple Easter craft with a deep meaning:

Use one-half sheet of construction paper folded in half and a few crayons.

On the front have each child draw a manger: Talk a little about Jesus' birth.
    Ask, "Is Jesus still there?"

On the next page have the children draw a cross. Talk a little about Jesus' death on the cross.
    Ask, "Is Jesus still there?"

On the third page, have the children draw the sealed tomb. Talk a little about how Jesus was buried in a borrowed tomb.
    Ask, "Is Jesus still there?"

Ask the children where Jesus is now. Help them to understand that they may invite Jesus to live in their heart. Draw a heart (a V with a 3 laying on it) on the last page.

Review the story so that the children can share the gospel using their card.

✤✤✤✤✤✤✤✤✤✤✤✤✤✤✤✤✤✤✤✤✤✤✤✤✤✤✤✤

 *Gems*

Choral Reading of the scriptures can be a tremendous blessing to the whole family.

Let each family member have a copy of the scripture (same version). Choose a chapter to read aloud in unison. Repeat this chapter until the children are almost reciting it from memory. Then choose a different chapter. Once a week review old chapters.

This will be a benefit to everyone's reading ability. Non-readers associate the spoken word with the printed word and begin to understand that reading is getting meaning from the printed page. Those just learning to read build skill and confidence and are not held back by not knowing every word. Average readers build speed, fluency and confidence. Everyone discovers joy in reading and enjoys doing something together and hearing the unison voices. Most of all, you are sinking the Scripture into their lives and bonding the family together and to the Lord.

Don't neglect this rich old-fashioned activity!

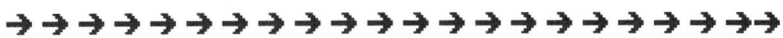 **Timeless Teaching Tips**

→→→→→→→→→→→→→→→→→→→→→→

Jesus took his learners away from the multitudes.

You represent Christ and His Plan.

Show the purpose of man and nations.

*The goal of a Christian education is to Glorify God,
build Christian character
and
raise up a godly generation.*

*God and His purposes never change.
His calling and gifts are never taken back.*

 *Gems*

****

Psalm 61:5
My heritage is not limited to blood relatives
of a generation or two.

**God is the Source of all authority,
law and government.
Authority, law and government
are defined in His Word.**

**God's Law must be written on the heart,
and government must FIRST begin internally.
If you are not self-governed,
no government will be able to control you!**

,n,n,n,n,n,n,n,n,n,n,n,n,n,n,n,n,n,n,n,n,n,n,n,n,n,n,n,n

It is given to you to understand mysteries. Luke 8:10

Jesus always taught face to face.
He taught, they practiced, they reported back.

****

 **Timeless Teaching Tips**

12345 23456 34567 45678 5678765 87654 76543 65432 54321

God's Purpose in Math:
To show His orderliness and design.

It would be interesting to search out the significance
of numbers and counting
in the Word.

Psalm 47:1
My people are destroyed for lack of knowledge (ABOUT GOD)

✧✧✧✧✧✧✧✧✧✧✧✧✧✧✧✧✧✧✧✧✧✧✧✧✧✧✧✧✧✧

Two areas should particularly testify of God:
Science - Seeing the Creator through His Creation
History - Understanding His Story;
seeing the Hand of God in and through
the People of God and their adversaries.

✦✦✦✦✦✦✦✦✦✦✦✦✦✦✦✦✦✦✦✦✦✦✦✦✦✦✦✦✦✦✦✦✦

Lay aside every encumbrance.

✦✦✦✦✦✦✦✦✦✦✦✦✦✦✦✦✦✦✦✦✦✦✦✦✦✦✦✦✦✦✦✦✦

 *Gems*

School

###

School is not just sitting at a desk with a book or a paper and pencil!
School is learning.
School is preparing for the future.
Learning involves doing.
School may be sorting hardware, sewing a doll dress, or setting the table for company. School may be writing a letter, labeling a photograph, or keeping a diary. School may be playing store, going to a museum, or learning to type. School may be grocery shopping, mowing the lawn or painting a bicycle. School may be teaching a brother to tie his shoes, babysitting the neighbor's dog or fixing the mower. School may be making a scrapbook, visiting an elderly neighbor, or fixing lunch. School may be reading a book to the toddlers, cutting pizza, or spreading jam on toast. School may be sharpening the pencils, straightening the room, or playing ball with a friend. School may be visiting the sick, making a card, or decorating the house. School may be counting acorns, drawing a princess or tracing a clown. School may be lessons in calligraphy, sewing, carpentry or Spanish. School may be learning to apply God's Word to every decision. School may also be learning to read, write and do arithmetic.

School is learning, doing and preparing.

Timeless Teaching Tips

==

We know a great deal about life in first century Pompeii because it was stopped and preserved in an instant by the eruption of a volcano.

We know even more about
the days of the War Between the States
because the average soldier kept a diary
and more than a million photographs were taken.

> How will future generations
> learn about our century?

Television? Newspapers? Magazines?
Tabloids? Novels? Art?

> Unless you and members of your family
> keep a diary or journal
> to pass on to the next generation,
> the main thing
> they will know about our era
> is the filth.

 *Gems*

☐ ☐ ☐ ☐ ☐ ☐ ☐ ☐ ☐ ☐ ☐ ☐ ☐ ☐

One-half inch graph paper is wonderful
for all kinds of things:

coloring inside the lines
printing lowercase letters
keeping math problems lined up (+, -, x, ÷)
teaching perimeter
teaching area
teaching the difference between area and perimeter
graphing progress

**Work from cause to effect.
Today's "history" seems to deal only with effect.**

The central theme of all of literature,
including drama and television,
is conflict.

Wisdom with obedience
yields peace with God
and resolves conflict.

✔ ✔

➡ Timeless Teaching Tips

Spiritual Considerations

How do I Bring My Children Up in the "Fear and Admonition of the Lord?"	225
Soaking in the Scriptures	227
Understanding the Bible – The Big Picture	230

Spiritual Considerations

How do I Bring my Children Up in the "Fear and Admonition of the Lord?"

1. Help them to see God in the daily little things. Take walks together and discuss everything you see, everything you feel. Answer every question in terms of God and His Word.

2. Teach them that there is a standard of right and wrong and

3. Teach them that standard.

4. Keep them in situations where that same standard is being observed.

5. Help them to see principles of truth upon which to base the decisions of life.

⇨ Timeless Teaching Tips

- Through how you make your decisions and defend why you allow or refuse permission for certain activities, hobbies, etc.
- In the literature you and they share (scriptures as well as other material).
- Stay away from places and literature and people where consequences are neither seen nor taught.

6. Teach them that obedience is not arbitrary, but love is. (They do not have to earn your love, it is always there; but they do have to win approval for the decisions they act out. Love does not have to be earned.)

7. Do not give undeserved praise or punishment, but lavishly share loving words and actions.

8. Rules do not depend on the whim of the rule maker. Some things are right or wrong no matter where, no matter who, no matter what.

Spiritual Considerations ✝

Soaking in the Scriptures

Do you want your children to love the scriptures? The language acquisition stage (up to about age seven) is wonderful time for building scripture memory and a deep seated love for the Word of God! During these years inundate your child with whatever you want him to know and believe in later years. Do you want him to know and love scripture? Introduce it now. Shakespeare? Classical music? Delight in the creation and its many aspects? Anger and bickering? Limits and "you can't." What your child hears and lives with now is what he will be comfortable with when he is older.

This is the best time in the world to develop the child's love for and familiarity with scripture for many reasons.

• Repetition is fun at this age.

• New sounds are delightful to young children.

⇨ Timeless Teaching Tips

- Long and hard syllables or fancy languages are no problem. They may not be able to repeat them, but they will enjoy hearing them.

- Tastes and individual preferences are still developing.

- This is the natural age to be developing and stretching language ability.

- Children this age want to please and be like their parents.

- The child is in the imprint stage of his life. What he spends time with is what will feel comfortable and familiar later.

- He has no preconceived notion of what society will or should think.

Knowing this, how to get started? Read and recite scriptures all through the day!

➢ After the bedtime story, read a chapter of scripture.

➢ At the table read or recite the same chapter every day for a week.

➢ Choose a different scripture for each activity which is a normal part of the day - breakfast, lunch, bath, dressing, etc. - and recite that scripture each day at the appropriate time.

➢ Sing the scriptures, especially the Psalms. The melody isn't as important as the doing. Just open the Bible, and think of "do, re, mi." Put the two together and go from there. Or,

Spiritual Considerations

better yet, put your most musical child in charge of this the first few times.

- Make posters or banners of scriptures and put them in conspicuous places.

- Make a scripture scrapbook and read it weekly.

- Write each scripture you successfully memorize onto a 3x5 card. Let the child draw a picture of the scripture on the back. Punch a hole in each card. Use a single notebook ring to keep the cards together and review them weekly.

You may not do all of these activities all the time. You may choose one or two for this year and a different one the next year. The important thing isn't the method you choose. The important thing is bathing your children daily in the word of God throughout their childhood! You wouldn't neglect washing their bodies. Wash their spirits as well!

⇨ **Timeless Teaching Tips**

Understanding the Bible - The Big Picture

It is often helpful to begin any study with the big picture. Many of us have difficulty teaching the Bible because we have never ourselves understood the big picture. It is rarely taught. Let's take a look at the Bible from a different perspective. Let's jog through Biblical history.

> **Old Testament:**
> **God loved.**
> **God made.**
> **Man failed.**
> **God rescued.**

The message of the Old Testament (OT) is simple. God created man to have a relationship with Him. He wants a person or a people to make the choice to fully serve Him and spread His name throughout the world. He started with Adam. Adam chose disobedience and suffered the consequences. When evil spread throughout the land, God saved only Noah's family from a destructive flood.

Spiritual Considerations

Later, God selected Abraham to start a nation. Through Moses He gave laws and rules to the nation of Israel. He promised to bless their obedience and punish disobedience. Obeying these laws

> **God's Goal: That the World Would Know that He is God.**

would make the people of the Hebrew nation both internally and visibly different so that God's vision might be filled: "that they (the world) might know that I am God."

First under a series of judges, then under kings, the nation of Israel failed over and over to live in strict obedience. They were finally conquered and scattered. The good news is that God did not ever totally forsake or destroy them. From the beginning, He had a plan for saving their physical and spiritual lives. The message of the New Testament (NT) is the story of the fulfillment of God's plan to save His people spiritually. Understanding the heart of God with His desire to make Himself known and the failure of man is essential to understanding the rest of history and our own purpose on earth.

The Bible is full of summaries of the Old Testament. My favorite summaries are Nehemiah 9: 7-35

> **Summarize the Bible**

and Psalm 105-106. In several places, including Acts 2: 22-40 and Romans 1:20-32, the New Testament summarizes its own message. This month read the summaries aloud. Have the older children look for other summaries or write their own. Discuss what God wanted from His people. Discuss the ways they failed. Discuss God's response to their failure - forgiveness over

⇨ Timeless Teaching Tips

and over, finally punishment, a plan for eternal salvation, the fulfillment of that plan.

Recall as many Bible people as you can. Retell as much of their story as you remember. List things they did right and what they did wrong. Discuss their character traits - both good and bad. What talents did they have that God used? Tell God's response, how God used them, or some lessons God wants us to learn from their lives. Make a book with a page or chapter for each person you discuss. Younger children could draw pictures and tell an older child what to write. Older children could write about each person. Adjust the assignment to fit the ability of the child. Do a person a day if this is your only history, or a person a week if it supplements other studies. Read Ezekiel 14: 14 and 20. Discuss the lives of these three people and include them in your book. Read the Hall of Fame in Hebrews 11. Include some of these men. Why are Abraham, David, and Joseph included in Hebrews 11, but not in Ezekiel 14?

Bring the Lesson Home.

Don't stop there. Ask, "So what?" What has this to do with my life today? Is God still looking for a person or people to follow Him whole-heartedly? (II Chronicles 6:9, Hebrews 13:8) Is it possible for me to be counted with Noah, Daniel, and Job? What is the challenge to me? Read Acts 13:22. How could a man who sinned as David did be said to be after God's own heart? What should I do when I sin? What character traits do I want to keep in my life? What skills do I have or can I develop that God can use? Am I willing to be used of God to spread His name and His glory? In prayer make yourself available to God to carry out His vision in front of and in the midst of the world today.